US FDA and Other International Drugs and Cosmetics Acts

US FDA and Other International Drugs and Cosmetics Acts

Ranjan Magazine
Plant Head
Manufacturing and Marketing
Sunny Allied Industries
Jammu, J&K

CBS Publishers & Distributors Pvt Ltd

New Delhi • Bengaluru • Chennai • Kochi • Kolkata • Mumbai
Hyderabad • Nagpur • Patna • Pune • Vijayawada

Disclaimer

Science and technology are constantly changing fields. New research and experience broaden the scope of information and knowledge. The author has tried his best in giving information available to him while preparing the material for this book. Although, all efforts have been made to ensure optimum accuracy of the material, yet it is quite possible some errors might have been left uncorrected. The publisher, the printer and the author will not be held responsible for any inadvertent errors, omissions or inaccuracies.

US FDA and Other International Drugs and Cosmetics Acts

ISBN: 978-93-86217-68-4

First Edition: 2017

Published by Satish Kumar Jain and produced by Varun Jain for

CBS Publishers & Distributors Pvt Ltd

4819/XI Prahlad Street, 24 Ansari Road, Daryaganj, New Delhi 110 002, India.

Ph: 23289259, 23266861, 23266867 Website: www.cbspd.com

Fax: 011-23243014 e-mail: delhi@cbspd.com; cbspubs@airtelmail.in.

Corporate Office: 204 FIE, Industrial Area, Patparganj, Delhi 110 092

Ph: 4934 4934 Fax: 4934 4935 e-mail: publishing@cbspd.com; publicity@cbspd.com

Branches

- **Bengaluru:** Seema House 2975, 17th Cross, K.R. Road, Banasankari 2nd Stage, Bengaluru 560 070, Karnataka
  Ph: +91-80-26771678/79 Fax: +91-80-26771680 e-mail: bangalore@cbspd.com
- **Chennai:** 7, Subbaraya Street, Shenoy Nagar, Chennai 600 030, Tamil Nadu
  Ph: +91-44-26680620, 26681266 Fax: +91-44-42032115 e-mail: chennai@cbspd.com
- **Kochi:** Ashana House, No. 39/1904, AM Thomas Road, Valanjambalam, Ernakulam 682 018, Kochi, Kerala
  Ph: +91-484-4059061-65 Fax: +91-484-4059065 e-mail: kochi@cbspd.com
- **Kolkata:** 6/B, Ground Floor, Rameswar Shaw Road, Kolkata-700 014, West Bengal
  Ph: +91-33-22891126, 22891127, 22891128 e-mail: kolkata@cbspd.com
- **Mumbai:** 83-C, Dr E Moses Road, Worli, Mumbai-400018, Maharashtra
  Ph: +91-22-24902340/41 Fax: +91-22-24902342 e-mail: mumbai@cbspd.com

Representatives

- **Hyderabad** 0-9885175004
- **Nagpur** 0-9021734563
- **Patna** 0-9334159340
- **Pune** 0-9623451994
- **Vijayawada** 0-9000660880

Printed at: Swastik Packagings, Patparganj Industrial Area, Delhi, India

Preface

This is an important book on international and national drugs and cosmetics Acts for the use of students, laboratory practice, pharmacists, formulators, marketers, and person in testing, manufacturing and marketing of drugs and cosmetics products. This book is updated, original and easy to study and implement. Everyday we see several persons trapped in criminal activities due to the fact that they are not aware about various acts. Such persons spoil their lives by undergoing imprisonment and fine by the court. Criminal activities are always a loss to person and nation because it spoils the image of person and nation. Drugs and Cosmetics Act is for the better life and prosperity of nation.

The objective of this book is to increase business of pharmacy products in the World. This Act provides safety to human but on the other part this Act increases the prices of pharmacy products for example in United Kingdom, there is no license for the manufacturing and marketing of herbal medicine. The idea is simply to make and sell monopoly pharmacy products at lowest price in the market for the benefit of consumers.

Ranjan Magazine
ranjan.magazine@gmail.com

Contents

1

United States of America

US FOOD AND DRUG ADMINISTRATION

A Brief History of Early Drug Regulation in the United States

The US Food and Drug Administration (US FDA) is the oldest federal agency dedicated to consumer protection, originating as a single chemist appointed to the US Department of Agriculture in 1862. FDA in 2006 employed more than 10,000 toxicologists, chemists, pharmacologists, physicians, microbiologists, pharmacists, veterinarians, lawyers, and others. This poster, excerpted from materials produced by the FDA's History Office highlights the fascinating early origins of the regulation of medicines and accompanies several objects generously loaned by the University of Arizona's Museum of Pharmacy.

Rising popularity of patent medicines or "Nostrums" in the 19th century

Throughout the 1800s, in an era of limited physician tools for treating illness that had been scrutinized and supported by empirical evidence and the scientific method, an increasingly urbane population in the United States developed an appetite for medical elixirs. Marketed through exoticism, mystery, and grandiose claims of efficacy, these medicines claimed to cure everything from cancer, venereal disease, female troubles, stomachaches, and epilepsy. One product sold widely in the late 1800s and early 20th century, William Radam's microbe killer, boldly declared on the label "Cures all diseases", while Dr Sibley advertised that his Solar Tincture was even able to "restore life in the event of sudden death." In fact, these products often simply relied upon opiates, cocaine, or alcohol to make imbibers feel better or "cured"; however, in many cases, they contained toxic ingredients such as acetanilide or cresyl phosphate (an organophosphate causing nerve paralysis).

The Great American Fraud and the Pure Food and Drugs Act of 1906

In the early 1900s, while famed muckraking journalist Upton Sinclair's publications detailed the horrific conditions of the meatpacking industry, some of his colleagues exposed the false claims, harmful ingredients, and market manipulation of nostrums and their producers. The most famous of these investigations was published in *Collier's* magazine by Samuel Hopkins Adams in a series entitled "The Great American Fraud," concluding in February, 1906, the same month Sinclair's *The Jungle* was published. Four months later, the first Federal Pure Food and Drug Act was published, prohibiting interstate commerce of adulterated and misbranded food and drugs.

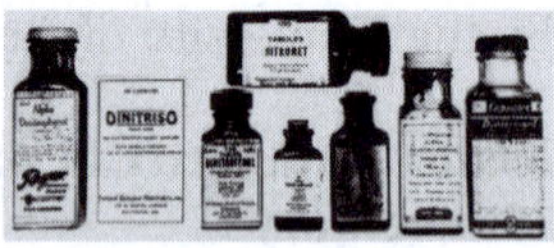

Though this led many patent medicines to remove narcotics instead of label them, it was less successful in corralling exaggerated claims or preventing many dangerous substances from reaching consumers.

The Sulfanilamide Disaster and The Federal Food, Drug, and Cosmetic Act of 1938

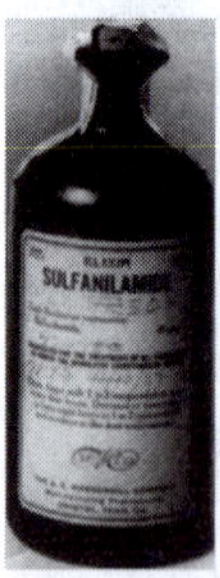

Between 1906 and 1938, legal proceedings over many problems with dangerous drugs demonstrated that the Pure Food and Drugs Act did not go far enough to protect public safety. In 1937, Massengill distributed an Elixir Sulfanilamide indicated for "all conditions in which the hemolytic streptococci appear." It contained diethylene glycol, a chemical analogue of antifreeze, leading to the documented deaths of 107 people, including many children. This disaster became the urgent impetus for the passing of the Federal Food, Drug, and Cosmetic Act. Among the Act's provisions were notably that all drugs be tested for safety prior to marketing, and the results submitted to the FDA in a new drug application (NDA).

It additionally authorized factory inspections, and required the establishment of safe tolerances for unavoidable poisonous substances.

Furthermore, FDA promulgates the policy in August that sulfanilamide and selected other dangerous drugs must be administered under the direction of a qualified expert, thus launching the requirement for **prescription only** (non-narcotic) drugs.

Timeline

1820 Eleven physicians meet in Washington, DC, to establish the US Pharmacopoeia, the first compendium of standard drugs for the United States.

1846 Publication of Lewis Caleb Beck's *Adulteration of Various Substances Used in Medicine and the Arts*, helps document problems in the drug supply.

1848 Drug Importation Act passed by Congress requires US Customs Service inspection to stop entry of adulterated drugs from overseas.

1903 Lyman F Kebler, MD, PhC, assumes duties as Director of the Drug Laboratory, Bureau of Chemistry.

1905 Samuel Hopkins Adams' ten-part exposé of the patent medicine industry, "The Great American Fraud," begins in Collier. The American Medical Association, through its Council on Pharmacy and Chemistry, initiates a voluntary program of drug approval that would last until 1955. To earn the right to advertise in AMA and related journals, companies submitted evidence, for review by the council and outside experts, to support their therapeutic claims for drugs.

1906 The original Food and Drugs Act is passed by Congress on June 30 and signed by President Theodore Roosevelt. It prohibits interstate commerce in misbranded and adulterated foods and drugs. The Meat Inspection Act is passed the same day. Shocking disclosures of insanitary conditions in meat-packing plants, the use of poisonous preservatives and dyes in foods, and cure-all claims for worthless and dangerous patent medicines were the major problems leading to the enactment of these laws.

1911 In US V Johnson, the Supreme Court rules that the 1906 Food and Drugs Act does not prohibit false therapeutic claims but only false and misleading statements about the ingredients or identity of a drug.

1912 Congress enacts the Sherley Amendment to overcome the ruling in US V Johnson. It prohibits labeling medicines with false therapeutic claims intended to defraud the purchaser, a standard difficult to prove.

1914 The Harrison Narcotic Act imposes upper limits on the amount of opium, opium-derived products, and cocaine allowed in products available to the public; requires prescriptions for products exceeding the allowable limit of narcotics; and mandates increased record-keeping for physicians and pharmacists that dispense narcotics. A separate law dealing with marijuana would be enacted in 1937.

1933 FDA recommends a complete revision of the obsolete 1906 Food and Drugs Act. The first bill is introduced into the Senate, launching a five-year legislative battle.

FDA assembles a graphic display of shortcomings in pharmaceutical and other regulation under the 1906 act, dubbed by one reporter as the Chamber of Horrors, exhibited nationwide to help draw support for a new law.

1937 Elixir Sulfanilamide, containing the poisonous solvent diethylene glycol, kills 107 persons, many of whom are children, dramatizing the need to establish drug safety before marketing and to enact the pending food and drug law.

1938 The Federal Food, Drug, and Cosmetic Act of 1938 is passed by Congress, containing significant new provisions requiring drugs to be proven safe before marketing. Under the Wheeler-Lea Act, the Federal Trade Commission is charged to oversee advertising associated with products, including pharmaceuticals, otherwise regulated by FDA.

1941 Insulin Amendment requires FDA to test and certify purity and potency of this life-saving drug for diabetes.

Nearly 300 deaths and injuries result from distribution of sulfathiazole tablets tainted with the sedative, phenobarbital. The incident prompts FDA to revise manufacturing and quality controls drastically, the beginning of what would later be called good manufacturing practices (GMPs).

1952 A nationwide investigation by FDA reveals that chloramphenicol, a broad-spectrum antibiotic, has caused nearly 180 cases of often fatal blood diseases. Two years later FDA would engage the American Society of Hospital Pharmacists, the American Association of Medical Record Librarians, and later the American Medical Association in a voluntary program of drug reaction reporting.

1955 HEW Secretary Olveta Culp Hobby appoints a committee of 14 citizens to study the adequacy of FDA's facilities and programs. The committee recommends a substantial expansion of FDA staff and facilities, a new headquarters building, and more use of educational and informational programs.

1962 Thalidomide, a new sleeping pill, is found to have caused birth defects in thousands of babies born in Western Europe. News reports on the role of Dr Frances Kelsey, FDA medical officer, in keeping the drug off the US market, arouse public support for stronger drug regulation.

Kefauver-Harris Drug Amendments are passed to ensure drug efficacy and greater drug safety. **For the first time, drug manufacturers are required to prove to FDA the effectiveness of their products before marketing them.** In addition, FDA is given closer control over investigational drug studies, FDA inspectors are granted access to additional company records, and manufacturers must demonstrate the efficacy of products approved prior to 1962.

1968 FDA Bureau of Drug Abuse Control and the Treasury Department's Bureau of Narcotics are transferred to the Department of Justice to form the Bureau of Narcotics and Dangerous Drugs (BNDD), consolidating efforts to police traffic in abused drugs. A reorganization of BNDD in 1973 formed the Drug Enforcement Administration.

FDA forms the Drug Efficacy Study Implementation (DESI) to incorporate the recommendations of a National Academy of Sciences investigation of effectiveness of drugs marketed between 1938 and 1962.

1970 In Upjohn V. Finch, the Court of Appeals upholds enforcement of the 1962 drug effectiveness amendments by ruling that commercial success alone does not constitute substantial evidence of drug safety and efficacy.

FDA requires the first patient package insert: Oral contraceptives must contain information for the patient about specific risks and benefits.

1972 Over-the-counter drug review initiated to enhance the safety, effectiveness, and appropriate labeling of drugs sold without prescription.

1982 Tamper-resistant packaging regulations issued by FDA to prevent poisonings such as deaths from cyanide placed in Tylenol capsules. The Federal Anti-Tampering Act passed in 1983 makes it a crime to tamper with packaged consumer products.

1983 Orphan Drug Act passed, enabling FDA to promote research and marketing of drugs needed for treating rare diseases.

1984 Drug Price Competition and Patent Term Restoration expedites the availability of less costly generic drugs by permitting FDA to approve applications to market generic versions of brand name drugs without repeating the research done to prove them safe and effective. At the same time, the brand name companies can apply for up to five years additional patent protection for the new medicines, they developed to make up for time lost while their products were going through FDA's approval process.

1987 FDA revises investigational drug regulations to expand access to experimental drugs for patients with serious diseases with no alternative therapies.

1988 The Prescription Drug Marketing Act bans the diversion of prescription drugs from legitimate commercial channels. Congress finds that the resale of such drugs leads to the distribution of mislabeled, adulterated, subpotent, and counterfeit drugs to the public. The new law requires drug wholesalers to be licensed by the states; restricts reimportation from other countries; and bans sale, trade or purchase of drug samples, and traffic or counterfeiting of redeemable drug coupons.

1991 FDA publishes regulations to accelerate reviews of drugs for life-threatening diseases.

1995 FDA declares cigarettes to be "drug delivery devices." Restrictions are proposed on marketing and sales to reduce smoking by young people.

1997 Food and Drug Administration Modernization Act reauthorizes the Prescription Drug User Fee Act of 1992 and mandates the most wide-ranging reforms in agency practices since 1938. Provisions include measures to accelerate review of devices, advertising unapproved uses of approved drugs and devices, health claims for foods in agreement with published data by a reputable public health source, and development of good guidance practices for agency decision-making.

Regulations

Major loopholes in US federal law allow the $50 billion cosmetics industry to put unlimited amounts of chemicals into personal care products with no required testing, no monitoring of health effects and inadequate labeling requirements. In fact, cosmetics are among the least-regulated products on the market.

This section explores what's being done to change the broken US system, and how other countries are leading the way in smarter laws that protect their citizens.

Federal Legislation: Current cosmetics laws in the US date back to 1938. We are working to change that with the Safe Cosmetics and Personal Care Products Act of 2013, and we need your help!

FDA Regulations: What authority does the FDA currently have to regulate cosmetics? Very little. The FDA does not review—nor does it have the authority to regulate—what goes into cosmetics before they are marketed to salons and consumers.

State Legislation: In the absence of federal oversight, states have taken steps to ensure that consumers have access to safer cosmetics and more information about the products they buy.

European Laws: Are companies making safer products in Europe than in the US? In some cases, yes, thanks to the European Union's stronger consumer health protections.

Canadian Laws: The Canadian government recently created a Cosmetic Ingredient Hotlist that includes hundreds of prohibited and restricted chemicals and contaminants.

Legislator Lookup: Do not know who your elected officials are? Look them up here (US only).

Safe Cosmetics and Personal Care Products Act

It is up to Congress to close gaping holes in the outdated federal law that allows **cancer-causing chemicals in baby shampoo, hormone disruptors in fragrance** and **lead in lipstick**. That is what you get when you have a $50 billion industry that is practically self-regulated.

The Safe Cosmetics and Personal Care Products Act of 2013 (HR 1385), introduced on March 21, 2013 by Reps. Jan Schakowsky, D-Ill. and Ed Markey, D-Mass, is designed to give the US. Food and Drug Administration authority to ensure that personal care products are free of harmful ingredients and that ingredients are fully disclosed.

Existing law—the Food, Drug and Cosmetic Act of 1938—cedes decisions about ingredient safety to the cosmetics industry. Under the current law, the FDA cannot require cosmetics companies to conduct safety assessments, and cannot even require product recalls. In a recent example, the FDA could not issue a mandatory recall of **Brazilian Blowout** hair straightening products even after they were found to contain formaldehyde.

Who will be Affected?

This legislation and subsequent reintroduction will affect every American—everyone who puts on moisturizer or uses shampoo or deodorant. More and more people are concerned about unsafe chemicals in our everyday lives, and getting these toxics out of the stuff we rub on our bodies everyday is just common sense. It will also help the cosmetics industry by fostering the development of the safer products American consumers are demanding.

Good for Consumers, Businesses, and Innovation

This legislation will be good for consumers, but it will also level the playing field for businesses that are making the safest products.

New advances in science have exposed the health risks of repeated exposures to **low-dose hazardous chemicals**—while also enabling green chemists to develop safer, non-toxic formulas. The cosmetics industry as a whole has not kept pace with safety innovations due to a weak regulatory system that encourages ignorance about chemical hazards and allows companies to hide the true toxicity of products.

What is in the Legislation?

Provisions of the Safe Cosmetics and Personal Care Products Act of 2013 include:

- Phase out of ingredients linked to cancer, birth defects and developmental harm.
- Creation of a health-based safety standard that includes protections for children, the elderly, workers and other vulnerable populations.
- Elimination of labeling loopholes by requiring full ingredient disclosure on product labels and company websites, including salon products and the constituent ingredients of fragrance.
- Worker access to information about unsafe chemicals in personal care products.
- Required data-sharing to avoid duplicative testing and encourage the development of alternatives to animal testing.
- Adequate funding to the FDA Office of Cosmetics and Colors so it has the resources, it needs to provide effective oversight of the cosmetics industry.

What You Can Do?

Ask your US Representative to **co-sponsor the Safe Cosmetics and Personal Care Products Act of 2013**. Congress needs to know that this issue is important to constituents!

Learn more about this issue and get your friends and family involved: Watch the short film, ***The Story of Cosmetics***, and share it with people in your life.

More Information

Press release: Toxic Chemicals in Cosmetics, Shampoos, Targeted by Congress (March 21, 2013).

Cosmetics manufacturers: What does the Safe Cosmetics and Personal Care Products Act mean for your business?

Fact sheet: The need for federal safe cosmetics legislation.

2

United Kingdom

Pharmaceutical Industry: Legislation, Guidance and Policy and UK MHRA

This page provides links to information on medicines legislation, guidance and policy. It includes an overview of medicines legislation, including preparing a medicinal product for sale in the UK or EU marketplace, how the Medicines and Healthcare Products Regulatory Agency (MHRA) develops policy, the 'Sunset Clause' (statutory requirements to inform the Licensing Authority of any disruptions in supply of medicines), and current MHRA consultations relevant to industry.

Overview of medicines legislation and guidance
Preparing a medicinal product for sale in the UK or EU marketplace
Herbal and homoeopathic medicines
Inspection
Importing and exporting
Pharmacovigilance
Borderline products
Advanced therapy medicinal products
Glossary of legislation
Review of medicines legislation project
Review of unlicensed medicines project
Sunset Clause

Does My Product Need a License?

Before a medicine can be placed on the UK market it must have a license (marketing authorisation) already granted, setting out its agreed terms and conditions of use such as indications and dosage. Obviously there are products where it is not easy to distinguish a medicine from, for example, cosmetics or food supplements. This section helps describe how a medicine is defined and how the Agency deals with such products that appear to fall within this borderline.

The MHRA also allows for certain exemptions from licensing. This section also outlines three of the more significant exemptions, i.e. the manufacture and supply of medicines for individual patients ('specials'); the import and supply of medicines for individual patients; and exemptions for herbal remedies.

Medicines That do not Need a License (Exemptions from Licensing)

The Human Medicines Regulations 2012 (SI 2012/1916) contains certain important exemptions from licensing and makes provision for further exemptions to be included in statutory orders. This section outlines three of the more important exemptions: The manufacture and supply of unlicensed relevant medicinal products for individual patients ('specials'), the importation and supply of unlicensed relevant medicinal products for individual patients, and herbal remedies exemptions.

The Manufacture and Supply of Unlicensed Relevant Medicinal Products for Individual Patients (Specials)

Medicines legislation (specifically The Human Medicines Regulations 2012 (SI 2012/1916)) requires that medicinal products are licensed before they are marketed in the UK. However, some patients may have special clinical needs that cannot be met by licensed medicinal products. So that these special needs may be met, the law allows manufacture and supply of unlicensed medicinal products (commonly known 'specials') subject to certain conditions.

The conditions are that there is a bona fide unsolicited order, the product is formulated in accordance with the requirement of a doctor, dentist, nurse independent prescriber, pharmacist independent prescriber or supplementary prescriber registered in the UK, and the product is for use by their individual patients on their direct personal responsibility. If a 'special' is manufactured in the UK, the manufacturer must hold a manufacturer's (specials) license issued by the MHRA. A 'special' may not be advertised and may not be supplied if an equivalent licensed product is available which could meet the patient's needs. Essential records must be kept and serious adverse drug reactions reported to the MHRA.

The MHRA Guidance Note 14, 'the supply of unlicensed relevant medicinal products for individual patients', provides guidance to manufacturers about the conditions under which they may manufacture and supply 'specials' and their legal obligations.

Contact for further information

For further information about the manufacture and supply of 'specials' for individual patients and the importation/export of unlicensed medicines, please contact the Policy Unit, Inspection, Enforcement and Standards Division, 151 Buckingham Palace Road, Victoria, London, SW1W 9SZ, telephone 020 3080 6131/6573/6595, email info@mhra.gsi.gov.uk

The Importation and Supply of Unlicensed Relevant Medicinal Products for Individual Patients

An unlicensed relevant medicinal product may only be imported into the UK in accordance with the provisions of The Human Medicines Regulations 2012 (SI 2012/1916). An importer must hold the appropriate wholesale dealer's or manufacturer's license that authorisers import (for details please see the MHRA Guidance Note 5 'notes for applicants and holders of a manufacturer's license' and Guidance Note 6, 'notes for applicants and holders of a wholesale dealer's license' for further information) issued by the MHRA and must comply with their license conditions. Importers' license conditions include the requirement that they must notify the MHRA on each occasion that they intend to import such a product. Importation may proceed unless the importer has been informed by the MHRA within 28 days that it objects to importation. The MHRA may object and prevent importation, because it has concerns about the safety or quality of the product, or because there is an equivalent licensed medicinal product available and it is not satisfied that there is a 'special need' for the supply to an individual patient.

An imported unlicensed relevant medicinal product may only be supplied in accordance with the Regulation 167 of The Human Medicines Regulations 2012 (SI 2012/1916). This exempts, under defined conditions (discussed in the previous section on 'specials') such a product when it is supplied to meet the 'special need' of an individual patient.

Notification of intention to import application form

Contacts for further information

For further information on wholesale distributors licenses, please contact the License Office, Inspection, Enforcement and Standards Division, 151 Buckingham Palace Road, Victoria, London, SW1W 9SZ, telephone 020 3080 6844 email info@mhra. gsi.gov.uk

For further information about notification of intention to import, please contact the Unlicensed Imports Section, 151 Buckingham Palace Road, Victoria, London, SW1W 9SZ, telephone 020 3080 7200, email info@mhra. gsi.gov.uk

Herbal Remedies Exemptions

Products exempt from licensing include herbal medicines which satisfy the conditions laid down in Regulation 241 12(1) only, 12(2) was revoked in 2011 of The Human Medicines Regulations 2012 (S1 2012/1916).

Regulation 8(1) of the Act defines a herbal medicinal product as "... a medicinal product consisting of a substance produced by subjecting a plant or plants to drying, crushing or any other process, or of a mixture whose sole ingredients are two or more substances so produced, or of a mixture whose sole ingredients are one or more substances so produced and water or some other inert substance".

Regulation 3(6) and (9) and Regulation 241 allows a person to make, sell and supply a herbal remedy during the course of their business provided the remedy is manufactured or assembled on the premises and that it is supplied as a consequence of a consultation between the person and their patient. Section 12(2) was revoked in 2011.

Contact for further information

For further information about herbal medicinal products exemptions, please contact the Herbal Medicines Policy Section, 5 Magenta, 151 Buckingham Palace Road, Victoria, London, SW1W 9SZ, telephone 020 3080 6404 or email info@mhra.gsi.gov.uk

SUMMARY

Cosmetic products are substances or mixtures of substances intended to be placed in contact with the external parts of the human body (epidermis, hair system, nails, etc.) or with the teeth and the mucous membranes of the oral cavity with a view exclusively or mainly to cleaning them, perfuming them, changing their appearance, protecting them, keeping them in good condition or correcting body odours.

Free movement of these products in the internal market is permitted if they comply with this regulation.

Market surveillance

A **responsible person** established in the community shall be designated for each product placed on the market. This person shall ensure compliance of the products with the rules set out in the regulation. In particular, they shall ensure compliance with requirements relating to human health, safety and consumer information. They shall maintain a product information file accessible to the public authorities.

In order to ensure product traceability, responsible persons shall identify the distributors to whom they supply the cosmetic product for a period of three years following the date on which the batch of the cosmetic product was made available to the distributor. The same applies to all other persons involved in the supply chain.

In case of **product non-compliance**, the responsible person shall take measures to render it compliant, withdraw it from the market or recall it to the manufacturing company in all Member States where the product is available. **Where the responsible person does not take all appropriate measures, the competent national authorities may take the necessary corrective measures.**

If a product which complies with the requirements of the regulation presents or could present a serious risk to human health, the competent national authority shall take all necessary provisional measures to withdraw, recall or restrict the availability of the product on the market.

Limitations for certain substances

The Annexes of this Regulation give a list of prohibited substances (Annex II) or restricted substances (Annex III) with respect to use in cosmetic products. Certain colorants (other than those in Annex IV), preservatives (other than those in Annex V) and UV filters (other than those in Annex VI) are also prohibited.

The regulation prohibits the use of substances recognised as carcinogenic, mutagenic or toxic for reproduction (classified as CMR), apart from in exceptional cases. It provides for a high level of protection of human health where nanomaterials are used in cosmetic products.

Consumer information

Product **labelling** contributes to consumer protection. Containers or packaging must bear written information in indelible, easily legible and visible lettering. This information concerns:

- The name or registered name and the address of the responsible person
- The country of origin for imported products
- The weight or volume of the content at the time of packaging
- A use-by date for products kept in appropriate conditions
- Precautions for use, including for cosmetics for professional use
- The batch number of manufacture or the reference for identifying the cosmetic product
- The list of ingredients, i.e. any substance or mixture intentionally used in the product during the process of manufacturing.

The language of the information shall be determined by the Member State where the product is made available to the end user.

Animal testing

Animal testing must be replaced by alternative methods. The regulation **prohibits the performance of animal testing in the European Union** for:

- Finished products
- Ingredients or combinations of ingredients.

The regulation also prohibits the placing on the European Union market of

- Products where the final formulation has been the subject of animal testing
- Products containing ingredients or combinations of ingredients which have been the subject of animal testing.

A derogation from the ban relating to placing products on the market shall be granted until 11 March 2013 in order to test repeated-dose toxicity, the effects of certain substances on reproduction and to study toxicokinetics.

In exceptional circumstances, Member States may request the Commission to grant a derogation, after consulting the Scientific Committee for Consumer Safety (SCCS), if an ingredient in wide use which cannot be replaced gives rise to serious concerns.

Committee procedure

The Commission shall be assisted by the Standing Committee on Cosmetic Products.

Context

This regulation recasts directive 76/768/EEC due to the many amendments made to it and the new amendments that were required.

The new regulation shall apply in 2013. However, some of its provisions will apply from 1 December 2010: They concern substances which are carcinogenic, mutagenic or toxic for reproduction (classified as CMR).

Key terms

- *Substance:* A chemical element and its compounds in the natural state or obtained by any manufacturing process, including any additive necessary to preserve its stability and any impurity deriving from the process used but excluding any solvent which may be separated without affecting the stability of the substance or changing its composition.
- *Toxicokinetics:* Study of the long-term effects of toxic substances in the body.

3

International GMPs

Drug Quality: GMP Implementation

The first modern code that could be considered to be good manufacturing practices (GMPs), as we recognize them today, were the regulations issued by the Canadian Specifications Board of the Supply and Services Department in 1957 (referred to as the Quad regulations) used to assure that drugs supplied to the Canadian Military met quality specifications. Following the success of that regulation, GMPs started being issued by regulatory agencies at a rapid pace—the US FDA issued its first version of the GMPs in 1963, with the current version of the US GMPs essentially being drafted in 1973 and issued in 1976. The British GMPs drafted in 1968 were finalized and issued in 1973, in a rush following the Davenport incident (previously referred to).

By the early 1980s, distinct GMP codes had been issued by over 25 different countries—sometimes following the basic US or British GMP in outline, but typically adding a local wrinkle to the requirements. Thus, for example the British and US codes required that when an error is made in data entered in a record, correction of the error shall constitute four steps: Placing a single line through the error, entry of the correct data alongside the original erroneous error, entry of the signature or the initials of the person making the change and the date that the change was made. The Australian GMPs added the requirement that in addition the reason the error had originally been made also needed to be entered in the record; the Japanese added the requirement that the strike out be made with two lines, drawn in parallel. With the exception of the Japanese code of GMPs, the GMP codes all followed the same style, had similar texts, and made approximately similar demands of pharmaceutical manufacturers in the control of manufacture and laboratory testing.

The exception to the almost uniform worldwide style and content of the GMPs issued in Japan, whose GMP regulations were, until the latest edition in 2002 unlike that of any other country. While discussing the same issues as all other GMP codes, the Japanese style of GMPs were that they resembled detailed job descriptions describing the duties and responsibilities of various members of key management staff in the pharmaceutical company. They described the role and function of the Manufacturing Control Manager, the Quality Control Manager and the Product Security Pharmacist. Japanese Product Security Pharmacist was effectively equivalent to the European "Qualified Person". When auditing Japanese pharmaceutical companies, I have found that the concept of GMP compliance as it is understood in the West is almost totally unknown. However, what the Japanese have is a passion, and yes passion is the correct word, for product quality that far surpasses anything encountered in America or Europe. Some examples are:

- Entry to a tablet packaging area in a Japanese company typically involves stripping off all street clothes down to underwear, donning freshly laundered plant uniform, and then having that uniform gone over with an adhesive roller to collect any non-viable particles that might be adhering to the outside of the uniform.
- The typical Japanese defect rate for cracked film coated tablets is 1 tablet in a million—no Western company that I have audited in 30 years comes anywhere close to such a rigorous quality level demand.
- The Japanese veneration and dedicated reverence to quality is illustrated in how Japanese companies react to a product complaints, where invariably the results of the compliant investigation are communicated to the person making the complaint by a personal visit to the complainant from the company's Vice President of quality, a recitation of the deficiencies found, and an explanation of what measures the company is implementing to prevent the occurrence happening again—a series of events that are common in

Japanese culture, but to which no Western company would even dream of doing.

Most countries revise and update their GMPs about every five years to keep up with changes in the industry and changes to manufacturing and testing technology. The great exception to this is the United States FDA, which has not substantially changed its GMP regulations since issuing them in 1976. FDA's response to this criticism is that such updating and changes are unnecessary as the first paragraph of the regulations under 'Scope' (Section 21CFR210.1 (a)) states that "The regulations set forth in this part and in parts 211 through 226 of this chapter contain the minimum current good manufacturing practices for methods to be used in ..... the manufacture, processing, packing, or holding of a drug". So when the US GMPs are criticized for not referring to the function of "quality assurance", or not requiring the company to perform "self-inspection", or for not defining the term "validation", FDA's response is that the regulations oblige the manufacturer to keep 'current', and that anyway the regulations promulgated are the 'minimum'. [Michael: Are not the recently issued (draft) Aseptic Processing Guidance and (Part 11) requirements, examples of major changes in FDA GMPs? No they are not but good point, keep reading.]

This requirement for US manufacturers and those world-wide exporting to the United States, to keep current, gives rise to the uniform reference to the US GMP as being the "current good manufacturing practice" regulations, or cGMPs. The statement that the regulations are a 'minimum' means effectively that just because the authorities have not recently added something (i.e. a given requirement) into the regulations, does not necessarily mean a firm is absolved from being responsible for any unwritten regulatory requirement. It is wise to remember this.

Although FDA is always talking at industry conferences about new revisions to the cGMPs being under consideration, these revisions never seem to come to fruition. FDA has however been very active in publishing guidelines for its own inspectors on how to interpret GMPs, and guidance documents for industry on how they should interpret the GMPs (for example the issuance in 2003 of guidances on Aseptic Processing

Electronic Record (Part 11) requirements. Additionally FDA maintains an extensive internet presence and its website is a mine of useful information on many aspects of GMP compliance—so much so that FDA has developed a portal to its web pages designed specifically for the use of the pharmaceutical industry, making it easier for the pharmaceutical industry to find information relating to FDA and GMPs (see http://www.fda.gov/oc/industry/default.htm).

Additionally under the provisions of the US Freedom of Information (FOI) Act, the findings of all FDA GMP inspections are available for public access, and a significant industry has grown up in Washington in providing FDA inspection reports and other FDA documents to the pharmaceutical industry. This is in marked contrast to the rest of the world, where the findings of GMP inspections are never routinely revealed. In comparison in the United Kingdom for a British inspector to reveal, or leak any findings during a pharmaceutical facilities inspection is a breach of the "Official Secrets Act" (the same act that makes it against the law to reveal what her Majesty the Queen had for breakfast this morning) and can result in the inspector spending 10 years in prison and facing a heavy fine. As such, the US pharmaceutical industry has a little excuse for not being able to keep up with FDA's latest thinking. In fact GMP compliance in the USA is often thought of as playing a game where the goal-post keep moving, and as such close monitoring of FDA through its website, through FOI, through GMP consultants, through attendance at industry-FDA conferences, and through the trade press is compulsory for any company wanting to ensure that it stays in compliance with the cGMPs.

The World Health Organization (WHO) also deemed, it useful to issue its own set of GMPs as part of a scheme for "Certification of the Movement of Pharmaceutical Products in International Commerce". When first issued in 1967, the WHO GMPs were not very demanding, much like the 1963 first version of the US GMPs, and could have been met with relative ease by most developing world manufacturers. They were however one of the first attempts to provide a basic outline of the minimum steps required in establishing a pharmaceutical manufacturing facility meeting acceptable standards. In 1988, the British Commonwealth Pharmaceutical Association attempted to issue a GMP code applicable to developing nations in the Commonwealth, but this attempt floundered on the issue of whether the lesser developed nations should be required to meet the standards of the more developed nations, a constant problem when attempting to formulate international GMP codes. In fact, there is a global disequilibrium of quality, and the relative development of a nation will dictate what level of quality (e.g. GMPs), it can afford, or sees as being relevant to its situation.

Interestingly it was the Northern European nations that gave the greatest impetus to implementation of the GMPs, and to elaboration and expansion of the concepts involved with GMPs. In the late 1980s they realized that having the written document (the GMP code) was insufficient in itself; implementation of the GMPs required both the written document, and a sound policy of enforcement. If countries were to save time and effort and not need to always inspect manufacturers in other countries, then they reasoned it would be useful if one country could have faith that the national inspectorate of the other country inspected in much the same way that they did, with the same philosophy and intensity of inspection. If this could be assured, then duplicative and costly re-inspections could be eliminated.

So was born the Pharmaceutical Inspection Convention (PIC) or more properly called "The Convention for the Mutual Recognition of Inspections in Respect of the Manufacture of Pharmaceutical Products". This country grouping was originally composed of the countries of the European Free Trade Association (EFTA). EFTA was the Western European countries that were not a part of the European Economic Community (EEC), which later evolved into the European Union. The initial members of PIC were the EFTA nations at that time: Austria, Denmark, Finland, Iceland, Liechtenstein, Norway, Portugal, Sweden, Switzerland and the United Kingdom.

The original goals of PIC were:

- Mutual recognition of inspections
- Harmonization of GMP requirements

- Uniform inspection systems
- Training of inspectors
- Exchange of information
- Mutual confidence.

And in achieving these goals they were extremely successful.

The great strength of the PIC is that twice a year joint discussions are held between GMP inspectors from all the PIC Member States to discuss and elaborate on specific topics within the GMPs and to derive a harmonized approach and understanding as to how the PIC inspectorates understand the technology and want to have the PIC GMPs implemented (which had been published when PIC was founded). These discussions often resulted in supplemental guidelines which proved useful to the inspectors, but also gave industry a good grounding in new science and technology, as well as insight into the inspector's ways of thinking.

Additionally the Pharmaceutical Inspection Cooperation Scheme (PICS) has published highly informative guides on various aspects of GMP implementation, among which are:

- Recommendation on Quality System Requirements for Pharmaceutical Inspectorates (PI 002-1)
- Recommendation: Guidance on Parametric Release (PI 005-1)
- Recommendation on Validation Master Plan, IQ, OQ, PQ, Cleaning (PI 006-1)
- Recommendation on Validation of Aseptic Processing (PI 007-1)
- PICS Guide to Inspections of Source Plasma Establishment and Plasma Warehouses (PI 008-1).

These documents, and an extensive library of other publications reflecting the presentations given, and discussions held, at the bi-annual PICS deliberations, are available on the PICS website at http://www.picscheme. org/pubs/pubs.htm

So successful was the PIC scheme that the European Economic Community (EEC) later to become the European Union realized fairly early after its first expansion in 1973 from its original 6-member states (Belgium, Germany, France, Italy, Luxembourg, Netherlands) to 9-member states when the PIC countries of Denmark, Ireland and the United Kingdom joined the EEC, that it would be useful for those EEC members who were not PIC members (often referred to as the "original European club") to join the PIC, and to adopt the PIC GMP Guideline as the official EU GMP guideline.

Due to legal technicalities, in order for these "original European club" countries to join the PIC, the PIC was forced to change its format from being a formal inter-governmental convention between member countries into an association of member national health authorities changing the PIC into the Pharmaceutical Inspection Cooperation Scheme (PICS) but this was a legal technicality and it did not slow down the PIC in the scope of the work it was coordinating. The EU is now about to become a grouping of 25 countries, covering a population of approximately 450 million people, with the stated goal of achieving the free movement of trade, including pharmaceuticals, between them. As such, a PIC format of all national inspectors performing their inspectors to a single recognized and harmonized standard makes eminent sense from the perspective of eliminating bureaucratic waste.

Recognizing these obvious advantages in inspection efficiency Canada and the United States have both begun discussions with the European Union on enacting a scheme termed the "Mutual Recognition Agreement (MRA)" that would allow the inspections by one country to be acceptable in the other. Thus, FDA inspectors would no longer need to travel to inspect in Finland, but could rely on the inspection report of a Finnish GMP inspector. In a study to determine the standards of GMP inspections throughout Europe, FDA determined that most countries had acceptable GMP inspection systems, but that those of Southern Europe (historically parts of the Holy Roman Empire—previously discussed) were below standard and would not be acceptable to FDA under an MRA. The EU responded that the EU was one trading block, and that FDA either accepted everyone (inspection reports from all 15-member states), or accepted nothing. The FDA chose the latter and despite much effort between FDA and the EMEA (the European Medicines Evaluation Agency), the mutual recognition of GMP inspections discussions floundered. Interestingly the Canadian Health Product and Food Inspection Branch (HPFBI) had no such qualms and an MRA is in place since February 2003 between the Canadian and European Union.

Despite the US FDA publicly stating that they are the "gold standard in GMP development and enforcement" (as stated by Ms. Stephanie Grey, then head of FDA's Office of Compliance, at a national PDA conference in 1998, and by other senior FDA staffers at other industry meetings in the USA and internationally), in fact it is the PIC that has expanded the scope and concepts of GMP the most worldwide.

The PIC has now significantly expanded beyond being a club of Western European nations, with several Eastern European nations having joined (Czech Republic, Hungary, Latvia, Romania, Slovak Republic), along with Australia, Canada, Malaysia, and Singapore, thus making PICS, a truly international grouping of nations. Additionally the US FDA and WHO maintain observer status within PIC.

The regionalization of GMPs has had such obvious advantages that other regional groupings have tried to emulate it, but with only marginal degrees of success. Written GMP guides exist but coordination of inspections to a uniform standard are fairly haphazard. Regional groupings with GMP codes are ASEAN (Association of South East Asian Nations), a grouping now consisting of Brunei Darussalam, Cambodia, Indonesia, Laos, Malaysia, Myanmar, Philippines, Singapore, Thailand, and Vietnam; and Mercosur, a South American grouping of Argentina, Brazil, Paraguay and Uruguay. It is anticipated that the much hoped for Free Trade Area of the Americas (FTAA) between the North American Free Trade Area (NAFTA), Central and South America might give impetus to a harmonization of GMPs within the Americas, probably dominated by the Canadian and the United States philosophy of GMP.

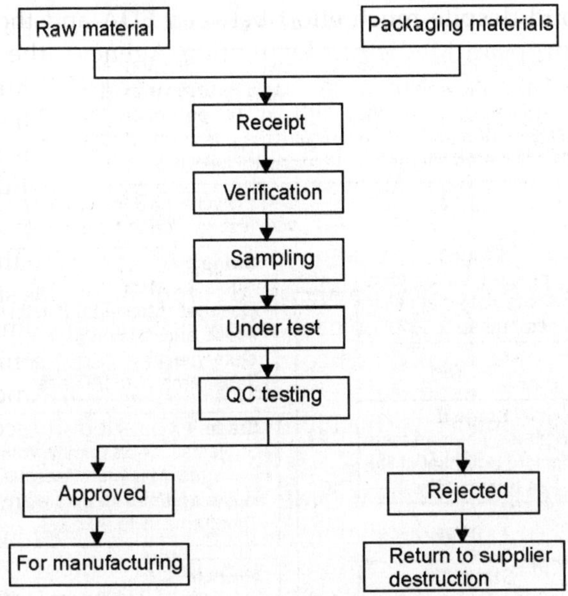
Raw material
Packaging materials
Receipt
Verification
Sampling
Under test
QC testing
Approved
Rejected
For manufacturing
Return to supplier destruction

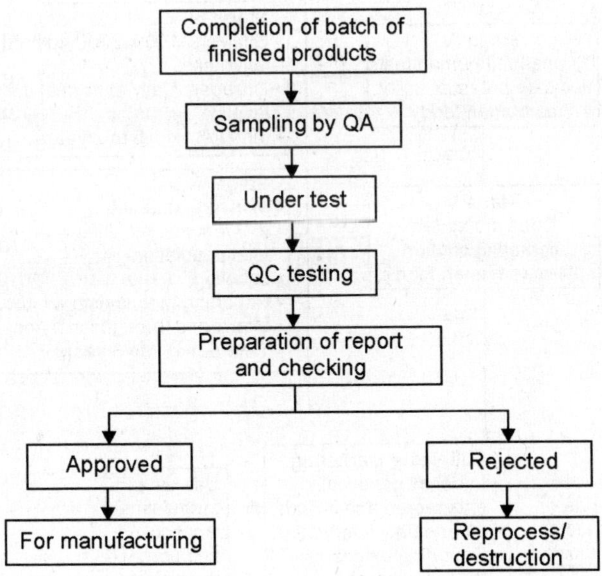
Completion of batch of finished products
Sampling by QA
Under test
QC testing
Preparation of report and checking
Approved
Rejected
For manufacturing
Reprocess/ destruction

XA Food Safey Assessment: Strategy IA emphasis on *in vivo* testing overview

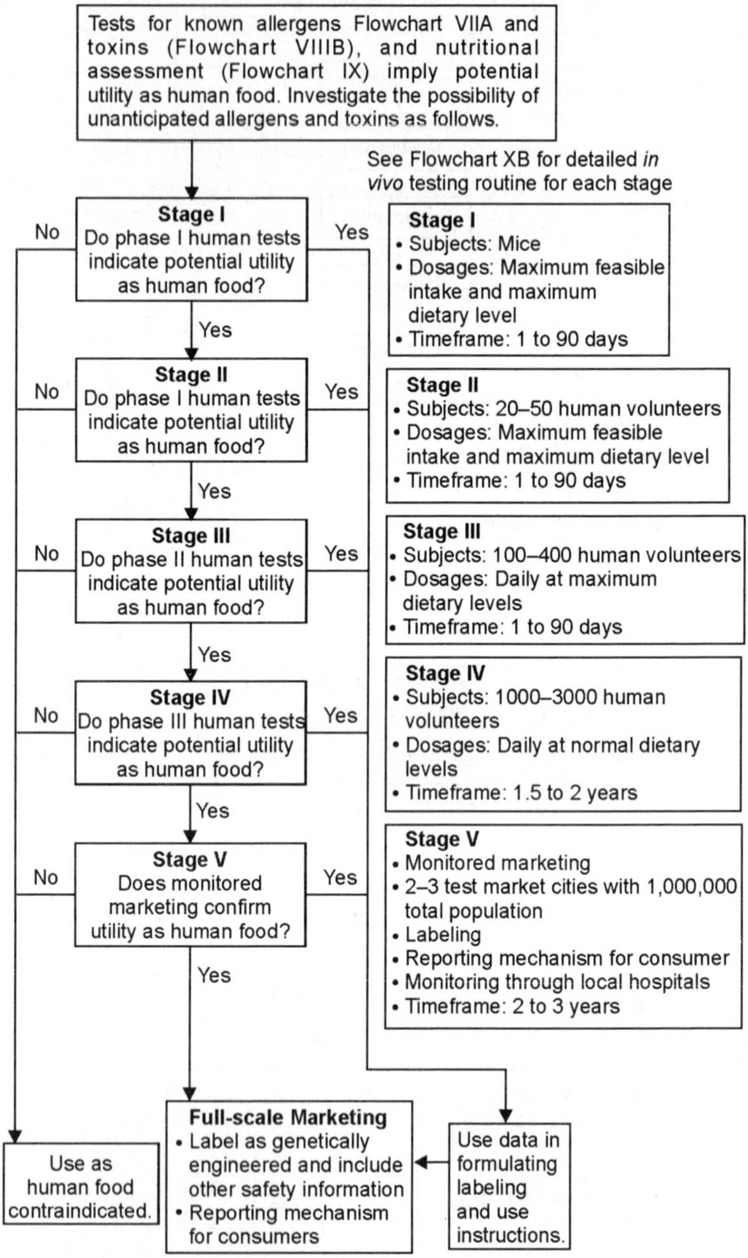

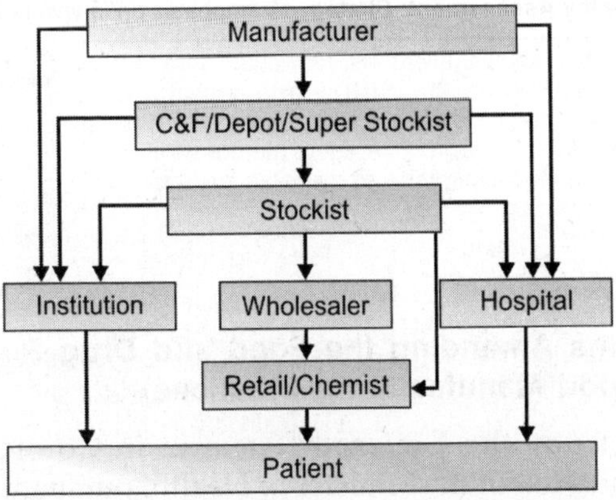
Manufacturer
C&F/Depot/Super Stockist
Stockist
Institution
Wholesaler
Hospital
Retail/Chemist
Patient

4

Canada

Regulations Amending the Food and Drug Regulations (1475—Good Manufacturing Practices)

His Excellency the Governor General in Council, on the recommendation of the Minister of Health, pursuant to Section 30[a] of the *Food and Drugs Act*[b], makes the annexed *Regulations Amending the Food and Drug Regulations (1475—Good Manufacturing Practices)*.

AMENDMENTS

1. **The definition "expiration date" in Subsection C.01.001(1) of the *Food and Drug Regulations*[1] is replaced by the following:**

   "expiration date" means

   a. in the case of a drug in dosage form, the earlier of the following dates, expressed at minimum as a year and month:
      i. the date up to and including which the drug maintains its labelled potency, purity and physical characteristics, and
      ii. the date after which the manufacturer recommends that the drug not be used

   b. in the case of an active ingredient, whichever of the following dates is applicable, expressed at minimum as a year and month:
      i. the retest date, or
      ii. the date after which the manufacturer recommends that the active ingredient not be used (*date limite d'utilisation*).

[a] SC 2012, c. 19, ss. 414(2) and 415
[b] RS, c. F-27
[1] CRC, c. 870

2. **(1) The definition "wholesale" in Subsection C.01A.001(1) of the Regulations is repealed.**

   (2) Subsection C.01A.001(1) of the Regulations is amended by adding the following in alphabetical order:

   "active ingredient" means a drug that, when used as a raw material in the fabrication of a drug in dosage form, provides its intended effect (*ingrédient actif*).

   "active pharmaceutical ingredient" means an active ingredient that is used in the fabrication of a pharmaceutical (*ingrédient actif pharmaceutique*).

   "bulk process intermediate" means an active ingredient that is used in the fabrication of either a drug of biological origin that is listed in Schedule C to the Act or a drug that is listed in Schedule D to the Act (*produit intermédiaire en vrac*).

   "wholesaler" means a person who is not a distributor described in Section C.01A.003 and who sells any of the following drugs other than at retail sale:

   a. a drug in dosage form that is listed in Schedule C or D to the Act or in Schedule F to these Regulations, or a controlled drug as defined in Subsection G.01.001(1);
   b. an active ingredient; or
   c. a narcotic as defined in the *Narcotic Control Regulations* (*grossiste*).

   (3) Subsection C.01A.001(2) of the Regulations is replaced by the following:

   In this Division and in Division 2, "drug" does not include a dilute drug premix, a medicated feed as defined in Subsection 2(1) of the *Feeds Regulations, 1983*, an active ingredient that is for veterinary use or a drug that is used only for the purposes of an experimental study in accordance with a certificate issued under Section C.08.015.

3. **Section C.01A.003 of the Regulations is replaced by the following:**

   C.01A.003. This Division and Divisions 2 to 4 apply to the following distributors:

   a. a distributor of an active ingredient or a drug in dosage form that is listed in Schedule C to the Act; and

b. a distributor of a drug for which the distributor holds the drug identification number.

4. **Subsection C.01A.004(1) of the Regulations is replaced by the following:**

C.01A.004. (1) Subject to Subsection (2), no person shall, except in accordance with an establishment licence,

a. fabricate, package/label or import a drug;
b. perform the tests, including examinations, required under Division 2;
c. distribute a drug as set out in Section C.01A.003 that is not an active pharmaceutical ingredient; or
d. wholesale a drug that is not an active pharmaceutical ingredient.

5. **(1) Paragraphs C.01A.005(*f*) and (*g*) of the Regulations are replaced by the following:**

f. whether the applicant proposes to carry out a licensed activity in respect of an active ingredient;
g. the address of each building in Canada in which the applicant proposes to fabricate, package/label, test as required under Division 2 or store drugs, specifying for each building the activities and the categories of drugs, and for each category, the dosage form classes, if any, and whether any drug will be in a sterile form.

(2) Subparagraph C.01A.005(*m*)(i) of the Regulations is replaced by the following:

i. the name and address of each fabricator, packager/labeller and tester of the drug and the address of each building in which the drug is fabricated, packaged/labelled or tested, specifying for each building the activities and the categories of drugs, and for each category, the dosage form classes, if any, and whether any drug will be in a sterile form.

(3) Paragraph C.01A.005(*n*) of the Regulations is replaced by the following:

n. in the case of any other importer, the name and address of each fabricator, packager/labeller and tester of the drugs proposed to be imported and the address of each building in which the drugs will be fabricated, packaged/ labelled and tested, specifying for each building the activities and the categories of drugs, and for each category, the dosage form classes, if any, and whether any drug will be in a sterile form.

6. **(1) Item 4 of Table I to Section C.01A.008 of the Regulations is replaced by the following:**

The table shows the item and the associated activities.

Item	*Activities*
4.	Distribute as set out in paragraph C.01A.003(*a*) a drug that is not an active pharmaceutical ingredient

(2) Item 7 of Table I to Section C.01A.008 of the Regulations is replaced by the following:

The table shows the item and the associated activities.

Item	*Activities*
7.	Wholesale a drug that is not an active pharmaceutical ingredient

(3) Table II to Section C.01A.008 of the Regulations is amended by adding the following after item 1:

The table shows the item and the associated activities.

Item	*Categories of drugs*
1.1	Active ingredients

7. **The Regulations are amended by adding the following after Section C.02.003:**

C.02.003.1 No person shall sell a drug that they have fabricated, packaged/labelled, tested or stored unless they have fabricated, packaged/labelled, tested or stored it in accordance with the requirements of this Division.

C.02.003.2 (1) No person shall import an active ingredient into Canada for the purpose of sale unless they have in Canada a person who is responsible for its sale.

(2) No person who imports an active ingredient into Canada shall sell any lot or batch of it unless the following appear on its label:

a. the name and civic address of the person who imports it; and
b. the name and address of the principal place of business in Canada of the person who is responsible for its sale.

Use in Fabrication

C.02.003.3 No person shall use an active ingredient in the fabrication of a drug unless it is fabricated, packaged/labelled, tested and stored in accordance with the requirements of this Division.

8. **Subsections C.02.012(2) to (4) of the Regulations are replaced by the following:**

(2) Every fabricator and packager/labeller, and subject to Subsections (3) and (4), every distributor referred to in paragraph C.01A.003(*b*) and importer of a drug shall maintain a system to ensure that any lot or batch of the drug fabricated and packaged/labelled on premises other than their own is fabricated and packaged/labelled in accordance with the requirements of this Division.

(3) Subsection (2) does not apply to a distributor if the drug is fabricated, packaged/labelled and tested in Canada by a person who holds an establishment licence that authorizes those activities in respect of that drug.

(4) Subsection (2) does not apply to a distributor or importer if the drug is fabricated or packaged/labelled in an MRA country at a recognized building and both of the following requirements are met:

a. the address of the building is set out in their establishment licence; and
b. they retain a copy of the batch certificate for each lot or batch of the drug that they receive.

9. **Sections C.02.013 and C.02.014 of the Regulations are replaced by the following:**

C.02.013. (1) Every fabricator, packager/labeller, wholesaler, distributor referred to in Section C.01A.003 and importer of a drug shall have on their premises in Canada, a quality control department that is supervised by personnel described in Section C.02.006.

(2) Except in the case of a wholesaler or a distributor referred to in Paragraph C.01A.003(*a*), the quality control department shall be a distinct organizational unit that functions and reports to management independently of any other functional unit, including the manufacturing, processing, packaging or sales unit.

C.02.014. (1) Except in the case of a wholesaler or a distributor referred to in Paragraph C.01A.003(*a*), no lot or batch of a drug shall be made available for further use in fabrication or for sale unless the person in charge of the quality control department approves the sale or the further use.

(2) A drug that is returned to its fabricator, packager/labeller, wholesaler, distributor referred to in Section C.01A.003 or importer shall not be made available for further use in fabrication or for further sale unless the person incharge of the quality control department approves the further sale or further use.

(3) No lot or batch of a raw material or packaging/labelling material shall be used in the fabrication or packaging/labelling of a drug unless the person incharge of the quality control department approves the use.

(4) No lot or batch of a drug shall be reprocessed unless the person in charge of the quality control department approves the reprocessing.

10. Subsections C.02.018(1) and (2) of the Regulations are replaced by the following:

C.02.018. (1) Each lot or batch of a drug shall, before it is made available for further use in fabrication or for sale, be tested against the specifications for that drug.

(2) No lot or batch of a drug shall be made available for further use in fabrication or for sale unless it complies with the specifications for that drug.

11. Sections C.02.019 to C.02.023 of the Regulations are replaced by the following:

C.02.019. (1) A packager/labeller of a drug, a distributor referred to in Paragraph C.01A.003(*b*) and an importer of a drug other than an active ingredient shall perform the finished product testing on a sample of the drug that is taken either

a. after receipt of each lot or batch of the drug on their premises in Canada; or
b. before receipt of each lot or batch of the drug on their premises in Canada, if the following conditions are met:
   i. the packager/labeller, distributor or importer
      - has evidence satisfactory to the Director to demonstrate that drugs sold to them by the vendor of that lot or batch are consistently manufactured in accordance with and consistently comply with the specifications for those drugs, and
      - undertakes periodic complete confirmatory testing, with a frequency satisfactory to the Director, and
   ii. the drug has not been transported or stored under conditions that may affect its compliance with the specifications for that drug.

(2) If the packager/labeller, distributor or importer receives a lot or batch of a drug on their premises in Canada, the useful life of which is more than 30 days, the lot or batch shall be tested for identity and the packager/labeller shall confirm the identity after the lot or batch is packaged/labelled.

(3) Subsections (1) and (2) do not apply to a distributor if the drug is fabricated, packaged/labelled and tested in Canada by a person who holds an establishment licence that authorizes that activity.

(4) Subsections (1) and (2) do not apply to a distributor or importer if the drug is fabricated, packaged/labelled and tested in an MRA country at a recognized building and both of the following requirements are met:

a. the address of the building is set out in their establishment licence; and
b. they retain a copy of the batch certificate for each lot or batch of the drug that they receive.

Records

C.02.020. (1) Every fabricator, packager/labeller, distributor referred to in paragraph C.01A.003(*b*) and importer shall maintain all of the following records on their premises in Canada for each drug that they fabricate, package/label, distribute or import:

a. except in the case of an importer of an active pharmaceutical ingredient, master production documents for the drug;
b. evidence that each lot or batch of the drug has been fabricated, packaged/labelled, tested and stored in accordance with the procedures described in the master production documents;
c. evidence that the conditions under which the drug was fabricated, packaged/labelled, tested and stored are in compliance with the requirements of this Division;
d. evidence that establishes the period during which the drug in the container in which it is sold or made available for further use in fabrication will meet the specifications for that drug; and
e. evidence that the finished product testing referred to in Section C.02.018 was carried out and the results of that testing.

(2) Every distributor referred to in paragraph C.01A.003(*b*) and importer shall make available to the Director, on request, the results of testing performed on raw materials and packaging/labelling materials for each lot or batch of a drug that it distributes or imports.

(3) Every fabricator shall maintain on their premises written specifications for all raw materials and adequate evidence of the testing of those raw materials referred to in Section C.02.009 and of the test results.

(4) Every person who packages a drug shall maintain on their premises written specifications for all packaging materials and adequate evidence of the examination or testing of those materials referred to in Section C.02.016 and of any test results.

(5) Every fabricator, packager/labeller and tester shall maintain on their premises in Canada detailed plans and specifications of each building in Canada where they fabricate, package/label or test drugs and a description of the design and construction of those buildings.

(6) Every fabricator, packager/labeller and tester shall maintain on their premises in Canada personnel records in respect of each person who is employed to supervise the fabrication, packaging/labelling and testing of drugs, including the person's title, responsibilities, qualifications, experience and training.

C.02.021. (1) All records and evidence of the fabrication, packaging/labelling, finished product testing referred to in Section C.02.018 and storage of a drug in dosage form that are required to be maintained under this Division shall be retained for one year after the expiration date of the drug unless the person's establishment licence specifies some other period.

(2) Subject to Subsection (4), all records and evidence of the fabrication, packaging/labelling, finished product testing referred to in Section C.02.018 and storage of an active ingredient that are required to be maintained under this Division shall be retained in respect of each lot or batch of the active ingredient for the following period unless the person holds an establishment licence that specifies some other period:

a. in the case of an active ingredient that has a retest date, three years after the lot or batch has been completely distributed; or
b. in any other case, one year after the expiration date of the lot or batch.

(3) Subject to Subsection (4), all records and evidence of the raw material testing referred to in Section C.02.009 and of the testing of packaging/labelling materials that are required to be maintained under this Division shall be retained for five years after the raw materials and packaging/labelling materials were last used in the fabrication or packaging/labelling of a drug unless the person's establishment licence specifies some other period.

(4) If a fabricator is required to maintain records and evidence in respect of the same active ingredient under subsections (2) and (3), they shall maintain them for the longest period that is applicable.

C.02.022. (1) Every wholesaler, distributor referred to in Section C.01A.003 and importer of a drug in dosage form shall retain records of sale of each lot or batch of the drug, which enable them to recall the lot or batch from the market, for one year after the expiration date of that lot or batch unless their establishment licence specifies some other period.

(2) Every distributor of an active ingredient referred to in Paragraph C.01A.003(*a*) and every wholesaler and importer of an active ingredient shall retain records of sale of each lot or batch of the active ingredient, which enable them to recall the lot or batch from the market, for the following period unless the person holds an establishment licence that specifies some other period:

a. in the case of an active ingredient that has a retest date, three years after the lot or batch has been completely distributed; or
b. in any other case, one year after the expiration date of the lot or batch.

C.02.023. (1) On receipt of a complaint or any information respecting the quality of a drug or its deficiencies or hazards, every fabricator, packager/labeller, wholesaler, distributor referred to in Section C.01A.003 and importer of the drug shall make a record of the complaint or information that contains the following:

a. the results of any investigation carried out under Subsection C.02.015(2) and, if applicable, the corrective action taken; or
b. the name and business address of the person in charge of the quality control department to whom the complaint or information was forwarded under Subsection C.02.015(2.1) and the date on which it was forwarded.

(2) Records referred to in Subsection (1) shall be retained for the following period unless the person holds an establishment licence that specifies some other period:

a. in the case of a drug in dosage form, one year after the expiration date of the lot or batch of the drug; and
b. in the case of an active ingredient,
   i. if the active ingredient has a retest date, three years after the lot or batch has been completely distributed, or
   ii. in any other case, one year after the expiration date of the lot or batch of the active ingredient.

12. **The Regulations are amended by adding the following after Section C.02.024:**

C.02.024. (1) Every distributor of an active ingredient referred to in Paragraph C.01A. 003(*a*) and every fabricator, packager/labeller, wholesaler and importer of an active ingredient shall add all of the following information to the documentation that accompanies the active ingredient, immediately after any like information that has been added by another person:

a. their establishment licence number, or if there is none, their name, address, telephone number, fax number and email address;
b. an indication whether they have fabricated, packaged/labelled, wholesaled, distributed or imported the active ingredient and the date on which that activity was carried out;
c. the expiration date; and
d. the lot number.

13. **Section C.02.025 of the Regulations is replaced by the following:**

C.02.025. (1) Every distributor referred to in Paragraph C.01A.003(*b*) and importer of a drug in dosage form shall retain in Canada, a sample of each lot or batch of the packaged/labelled drug for one year after the expiration date of the drug unless their establishment licence specifies some other period.

(2) Subject to Subsection (4), the fabricator of a drug in dosage form shall retain a sample of each lot or batch of raw materials used in the fabrication for two years after the materials were last used in the fabrication unless their establishment licence specifies some other period.

(3) Subject to Subsection (4), the fabricator of an active ingredient shall retain a sample of each lot or batch of it for the following period unless their establishment licence specifies some other period:

a. in the case of an active ingredient that has a retest date, three years after the lot or batch has been completely distributed; or
b. in any other case, one year after the expiration date of the lot or batch.

(4) If a fabricator is required to maintain samples in respect of the same active ingredient under Subsections (2) and (3), they shall maintain them for the longest period that is applicable.

14. Sections C.02.027 and C.02.028 of the Regulations are replaced by the following:

C.02.027. (1) Every distributor referred to in Paragraph C.01A.003(*b*) and importer of a drug in dosage form shall establish the period during which each drug in the package in which it is sold will comply with the specifications for that drug.

(2) Every fabricator and importer of an active ingredient shall establish the period during which each drug in the package in which it is sold will comply with the specifications for that drug.

C.02.028. (1) Every distributor referred to in paragraph C.01A.003(*b*) and importer of a drug in dosage form shall monitor, by means of a continuing program, the stability of the drug in the package in which it is sold.

(2) Every fabricator and importer of an active ingredient shall monitor, by means of a continuing program, the stability of the drug in the package in which it is sold.

15. The definition "drug" in Section C.03.001 of the Regulations is replaced by the following:

"drug" means a drug that is listed in Schedule C to the Act that is in dosage form or a drug that is an active ingredient of biological origin that can be used in the preparation of a drug listed in that Schedule (*drogue*).

16. The definition "drug" in Section C.04.001 of the Regulations is replaced by the following:

"drug" means a drug that is listed in Schedule D to the Act that is in dosage form or a drug that is an active ingredient that can be used in the preparation of a drug listed in that Schedule (*drogue*).

Transitional Provisions

17. (1) Every person who, on the day on which these Regulations come into force, fabricates, packages/labels, tests or imports an active pharmaceutical ingredient may continue to do so without an establishment licence if they submit an application for a licence under Section C.01A.005 of the *Food and Drug Regulations* within three months after that day.

(2) Subsection (1) applies until the determination of the licence application under Section C.01A.008 or C.01A.010 of the *Food and Drug Regulations*.

18. The *Food and Drug Regulations*, as they read immediately before the coming into force of these Regulations, continue to apply in respect of whole blood and blood components for a period of one year after the day on which these Regulations come into force.

Coming into Force

19. These Regulations come into force six months after the day on which they are published in the *Canada Gazette*, Part II.

Regulatory Impact Analysis Statement

(*This statement is not part of the Regulations.*)

Executive Summary

Issues: The quality of active ingredients (AI) in a drug has a direct effect on the safety and efficacy of that drug. Poorly manufactured and contaminated AI have been associated with negative health outcomes, including death, in a number of incidents over the past decades. Worldwide, there has been growing concern over the quality of AI as the manufacturing of AI and dosage-form drugs has been increasingly outsourced to developing countries.

In 2000, the international community of pharmaceutical regulators and manufacturers developed and adopted a guideline concerning good manufacturing practices (GMP) for AI. In the years since the guideline was finalized, most of the industrialized world has implemented the guideline in law. These Regulations will make GMP for AI, a regulatory requirement in Canada as well, helping to ensure the quality of AI in drugs available to Canadians and bringing Canada into line with its international regulatory counterparts.

Description: These Regulations will extend the drug GMP requirements set out in the *Food and Drug Regulations* such that they apply to all AI; extend the drug establishment licensing (EL) requirements set out in the *Food and Drug Regulations* such that they apply to all AI fabricators, packagers/labellers, testers and importers; and create a new record-keeping requirement to foster the traceability of AI from the original fabricator to the dosage-form drug manufacturer.

Cost-benefit statement: These Regulations will provide a net benefit to Canadians, with a net present value (NPV) of about $33.4 million over 10 years. The quantified benefits relate primarily to cost savings to industry due to removal of poor-quality drug products at the AI stage instead of recalls at the dosage-form stage. The qualitative benefits relate primarily to better protection for Canadians from poor-quality drug products.

"One-for-One" Rule and small business lens: The "One-for-One" Rule applies to these Regulations. Specifically, the administrative burden is estimated to have an annualized "IN" value of $58,500. The small business lens requirements do not apply to these Regulations as the annual average regulatory burden (compliance and administrative costs) to industry of the Regulations is estimated to be $196,000, well below the threshold of $1 million.

Domestic and international coordination and cooperation: These Regulations will allow Canada to establish regulatory equivalence in respect of AI with other industrialized countries, particularly those with which Canada has a Mutual Recognition Agreement (MRA). This will reduce duplicative regulatory oversight, facilitate participation by Canadian manufacturers in the international pharmaceutical market, and allow Health

Canada to reciprocate in international regulatory work-sharing to ensure the safety of the global AI supply.

Issue

Active ingredients (AI) are substances or mixture of substances that, when used as a raw material in the fabrication of a drug in dosage form, provide the intended effect. The AI contained in most pharmaceuticals are chemical in origin and are often referred to as active pharmaceutical ingredients (API). Examples would include the acetaminophen contained in a pain relief tablet, or the sildenafil citrate contained in an erectile dysfunction drug. AI of biological origin are often referred to as bulk process intermediates (BPI). One example would be the insulin contained in an insulin pen cartridge, for use by diabetics.

The quality of the AI in a drug has a direct effect on the safety and efficacy of that drug. Poorly manufactured and contaminated AI have been associated with negative health outcomes, including death, in a number of incidents over the past decades. A recent example is the 2008 international crisis regarding contaminated heparin, a blood-thinning drug. An investigation by the US Food and Drug Administration (FDA) revealed that bulk heparin sodium (an AI) purchased from an Asian supplier by the US drug manufacturer was contaminated with oversulfated chondroitin sulphate (OSCS). As of April 29, 2008, the FDA associated 81 deaths and 785 serious injuries in the United States with tainted doses of heparin.[2] Worldwide, there has been growing concern over the quality of AI as the manufacturing of AI and dosage-form drugs has been increasingly outsourced to developing countries.

In Canada, the quality of drugs in dosage form and higher-risk AI (namely BPI) is ensured through, among other things, the imposition of good manufacturing practices (GMPs). GMPs

[2] Four lots of contaminated heparin, manufactured by another company but using AI supplied by the same firm, were also discovered in Canada and recalled in March 2008. No increase in heparin-related adverse reactions were reported to Health Canada. It is possible that the recalled Canadian products had lower levels of contamination, reached fewer patients, or were formulated differently from the recalled US products. There may also be different practices or tendencies relating to adverse reaction reporting in the two countries.

ensure that products are consistently produced and controlled according to quality standards. However, there are no GMP requirements for API, the AI used in most pharmaceuticals. Current regulatory requirements pertaining to such AI mostly involve testing before use in a dosage-form drug, which cannot eliminate all risks.[3] Testing is also incapable of retroactively improving the quality of a product—an AI which has failed testing must either be destroyed without recovery of the cost of manufacture, or sold into a market which will accept substandard AI (e.g. a country with poor or no regulatory control over drugs, or a counterfeit drug ring).

In 2000, in recognition of the risks posed by poorly manufactured AI in a globalized pharmaceutical market, the international community of pharmaceutical regulators and manufacturers developed and adopted a guideline concerning GMP for AI, known as International Conference on Harmonisation (ICH) guideline Q7. In the years since ICH guideline Q7 was finalized, most of the industrialized world, including the United States, the European Union, Japan, Singapore and Australia, has implemented the guideline in law.

These Regulations will make GMP for all AI, a regulatory requirement in Canada as well, helping to ensure the quality of AI that are used in drugs available to Canadians, whether imported or domestically manufactured.

By bringing Canada into line with its international regulatory counterparts, the Regulations will also allow Canada to establish regulatory equivalence in respect of AI with other industrialized countries, particularly those with which it has a Mutual Recognition Agreement (MRA).[4] In evaluating the safety of AI

---

[3] For example, there was no test for OSCS prior to the 2008 heparin crisis.

[4] Canada currently has MRAs with the regulatory authorities of Austria, Belgium, Cypress, Czech Republic, Denmark, Estonia, Finland, France, Germany, Greece, Hungary, Ireland, Italy, Malta, Netherlands, Portugal, Slovak Republic, Spain, Sweden, United Kingdom, Switzerland, Iceland, Liechtenstein, Norway, and Australia. The MRAs relate to the parties' respective GMP compliance programs for drug products, allowing each regulator party to the agreement to accept the others' GMP inspection results as equivalent to its own. It is expected that equivalence in respect of AI could be established fairly rapidly, using existing MRA procedures, once the Regulations are implemented.

manufactured outside of Canada, Health Canada will be able to take advantage of GMP inspections by trusted international partners. Conversely, Canadian manufacturers will be able to leverage their compliance with Canadian requirements and inspection results from Health Canada to participate in the international drug market. Finally, Health Canada will be able to reciprocate in international regulatory work-sharing, joining ongoing programs[5] with other regulators to inspect AI manufacturing sites located in developing countries, and otherwise doing its part to ensure the safety of the global AI supply.

Objectives

The main objective of the Regulations is to protect the health and safety of Canadians by implementing into regulation internationally accepted GMP for AI requirements. A secondary objective is to ensure that the associated regulatory burden is mitigated by compensating efficiencies or minimized to the extent possible.

Description

The enabling legislation is the *Food and Drugs Act*. These Regulations will amend the *Food and Drug Regulations* as follows.

Good manufacturing practices requirements

The Regulations will generally impose on the fabrication, packaging/labelling, testing, storing and transport of all AI, the GMP requirements which currently apply to dosage-form drugs and the subset of AI known as BPI. This will be accomplished through the amendment of the definition of "drug" for the purposes of Division 2 of Part C of the *Food and Drug Regulations*. The Regulations will also amend or add provisions tailored to AI in accordance with ICH guideline Q7 where necessary (e.g. adding AI-specific record retention periods).

[5] The United States, the European Union and Australia are currently carrying out a pilot program, sharing inspection reports and carrying out joint inspections of foreign AI manufacturers.

Under the Regulations, no person who has fabricated, packaged/labelled, tested or stored a drug will be permitted to sell the drug unless they have performed their activity in accordance with GMP requirements. Dosage-form fabricators will be required to use only GMP-compliant AI in their drugs. A Drug Identification Number (DIN)-holding distributor or importer of a dosage-form drug will be prohibited from selling the drug unless it—including any AI used in it, are GMP-compliant.

The Regulations will carry out the main objective of improving the quality of AI used in drugs in Canada by implementing into regulation internationally accepted GMP for AI requirements.

Establishment licensing requirements

The Regulations will extend establishment licensing (EL) requirements to all AI fabricators, packagers/labellers, testers and importers. As with current EL holders, an EL will not be issued until the applicant has been assessed by Health Canada and found to be in compliance with GMP requirements.

Distributors and wholesalers of the subset of AI known as API, which only store and transport already-packaged and already-labelled API, will be subject to the applicable GMP requirements but will not be required to apply for an EL, as the risks do not warrant the imposition of an EL requirement and accompanying inspection program.[6] Dosage-form and BPI distributors and wholesalers will continue to be subject to EL requirements.

The Regulations will thus provide Health Canada with oversight and enforcement authorities regarding the riskiest activities in the AI supply chain, while ensuring the regulatory burden is not extended unnecessarily.

[6]Currently, distributors and wholesalers of BPI are subject to EL requirements because the risks incurred by improper storage and transportation are fairly high. BPI tend to be living organisms that can be killed, or have their nature radically changed, by small fluctuations in temperature, humidity, pH level, or stability (e.g. shaking). By contrast, while the storage and transportation of API are not without risk (hence the need for GMP requirements), finished API in sealed containers are able to withstand greater environmental fluctuation without effect.

Traceability requirement

Every fabricator, packager/labeller, distributor, wholesaler and importer of an AI, whether an API or a BPI, will be required to include, on the container label or on other documentation accompanying the drug, directly following the information provided by any previous party (*a*) the regulated party's name, contact details, and EL number, if applicable; (*b*) whether it has fabricated, packaged/labelled, distributed, wholesaled or imported the drug; (*c*) the date of that activity; (*d*) the expiration or re-test date of the drug; and (*e*) the lot number of the drug.

This record-keeping amendment fostering the traceability of AI will help to protect the health and safety of Canadians in several ways. It will allow for more rapid and targeted investigation and recall of problematic AI. It will also make the introduction of illegitimate, substandard AI into the supply chain more difficult as verification of an AI's provenance will be simplified.

The anticipated burden of this new requirement will be minimized to the extent possible by requiring only basic, easily available information from each regulated party, and by being nonprescriptive in terms of the format of the documentation. The burden will also be offset by the greater efficiency it will lend to both Health Canada when carrying out regulatory actions, and other regulated parties in complying with their obligations (such as the dosage-form manufacturer's obligation to verify the GMP compliance of the AI they use). Such transparency in the Canadian AI supply chain will also help to foster international confidence in the Canadian drug industry generally.

Transition period

The Regulations will come into force six months after the day on which they are published in the *Canada Gazette*, Part II. This delay in the coming into force of the Regulations will allow all regulated parties to adjust to the new requirements. Furthermore, on the day the Regulations come into force, any person who fabricates, packages/labels, tests or imports an API will be allowed to continue to do so without an EL provided they submit an EL application within three months after the coming into force of the Regulations. This transition provision will ensure that regulated parties do not find themselves in a state of non-compliance solely due to any Health Canada administrative delays.

Miscellaneous

Veterinary drugs: AI included solely in drug products for veterinary use are not within the scope of the Regulations.

Natural health products: As with veterinary drugs, AI included solely in natural health products are not within the scope of the regulations.

Whole blood and blood components: Until the new *Blood Regulations* are made, existing requirements, as they read immediately before the coming into force of the *Regulations Amending the Food and Drug Regulations (1475—Good Manufacturing Practices),* will continue to apply to whole blood and blood components.

Regulatory and Non-regulatory Options Considered

The following regulatory and non-regulatory options were considered.

Option 1: Status quo

Currently, API (a subset of AI) are not subject to any direct regulatory requirements other than the requirement for dosage-form fabricators to test a sample of each lot or batch of raw material against its specifications. The only assessment by Health Canada of API quality takes place during the pre-market drug submission review. The pre-market assessment provides an evaluation of the quality of the proposed API at the time of the application to market the dosage-form drug, but the evaluation is focused on the API's chemical properties and method of manufacture, and does not cover critical GMP areas such as quality management, facilities, and materials management (among others). This approach does not provide for oversight once manufacturing is underway.

A benefit of this option is that no additional financial costs for Health Canada or for regulated parties would be incurred. However, it constitutes an ongoing risk to the health and safety of Canadians. Also, under this option, Canada continues to be unable to participate in international regulatory cooperation to ensure the safety of the global AI supply, and Canadian industry continues to face barriers to entry into the global drug market.

Option 2: More active and ongoing promotion of the voluntary implementation of GMP for AI.

Health Canada guidance documents currently recommend voluntary implementation of ICH guideline Q7. Option 2 differs from Option 1 (status quo) in that it would involve more active and ongoing promotion by Health Canada of GMP for AI on a voluntary basis.

Knowledge of the benefits of GMP for AI is currently well disseminated throughout industry. Most Canadian companies which voluntarily comply with ICH guideline Q7 do so for the purposes of fulfilling the requirements of foreign regulatory authorities and business partners. These companies have some difficulty being inspected or audited for compliance, sometimes needing to arrange and pay for "foreign" inspections from their target markets, which puts them at a disadvantage compared to companies based in jurisdictions which have implemented requirements for, and inspect against, GMP for AI. Companies which sell only in Canada and which have voluntarily adopted ICH guideline Q7 as a best practice, to the benefit of Canadians, may be at a competitive disadvantage compared to other non-exporting companies which have chosen not to incur the additional cost of following ICH guideline Q7.

It is doubtful that further promotion by Health Canada at this point would motivate more of the Canadian AI industry to voluntarily adopt GMP. Under Option 2, Canadian companies which do not undertake foreign inspections would continue to be unable to participate in the international pharmaceutical market, and Canada would continue to be unable to participate in international regulatory cooperation to ensure the safety of the global AI supply.

Option 3: Regulatory amendment

Under this recommended option, following GMP for AI will become mandatory for Canadian industry and enforceable by Health Canada. Such a regulatory approach is consistent with Canada's current regulatory framework, which imposes GMP requirements for dosage-form drugs and BPI (AI of biological origin). The approach is also consistent with the approach taken by many of Canada's international regulatory counterparts, including the European Union, the United States, Japan, Singapore and Australia. A regulatory approach will allow for the extension of existing MRA arrangement to apply also to AI, and permit Health Canada to engage in international regulatory work-sharing in respect of GMP for AI inspections.

At some point in the future, Health Canada may consider the merits of developing a regulatory amendment to recover from industry some of the cost of conducting inspections by imposing EL fees similar to those currently in place for dosage-form drugs and BPI.

Benefits and Costs

Cost-benefit statement

As AI of biological origin (BPI) are already regulated in Canada due to their higher risk nature, the focus of the cost-benefit analysis is primarily on API. As indicated in the cost-benefit analysis, the Regulations will provide a net benefit to Canadians, with a net present value (NPV) of about $33.4 million over 10 years. The complete cost-benefit analysis is available upon request.

		Base year	Final year[7]	Total (PV)[8]	Annual average
A. Quantified impacts ($)					
Benefits	Industry—"Foreign" inspection fees savings for Canadian manufacturers selling abroad.[9]	$0.7M	$1.6M[10]	$8.9M	$1.3M
	Industry—cost savings due to removal of poor quality drug products at API stage instead of dosage-form stage.[11]	$2.4M[12]	$5.6M	$34.4M	$4.9M
	Total benefits	**$3.1M**	**$7.2M**	**$43.3M**	**$6.2M**

Contd.

[7] Year 2022.

[8] Discount rate of 7% as recommended by Treasury Board.

[9] It is a conservative figure based on the assumption that there are a minimum of 310 firms selling aboard (FDA data) and European Directorate for the Quality of Medicines (EDQM) & Health Care inspections are done at least once every three years (Health Canada estimate); no US fees are taken into account. The amount reflects the transition period, or 50% of the full year cost that could be charged by EDQM.

[10] Assumption of annual increase 2% in fees.

[11] It is a conservative figure based on the assumption that there are an average of 193 recalls of drugs in dosage-form annually, where 2–8% (5% being the median) of these recalls are API-related. Assuming the recall cost to industry is $1 million per recall, which is likely to be on the low end of the spectrum, there should be savings if the recalls were to be triggered earlier by API inspection or audit, before further investments are made to incorporate the substandard products into the final dosage form. The calculation uses generic oral solids as the baseline, which have a lower rate of saving as API constitute a higher proportion of their total cost (40–50%). Alternatively, one could argue GMP for API could prevent the quality defects leading to recall from occurring in the first place, which would provide a benefit of between $3.8 million and $15.4 million annually.

[12] The amount reflects the transition period, or 50% of the full year savings.

		Base year	Final year	Total (PV)	Annual average
A. Quantified impacts ($) (Contd.)					
Costs	Industry—training and administration costs for API fabricators, packagers/labellers, testers, importers, distributors and wholesalers.	$1.0M[13]	<$0.1M	$1.4M	<$0.2M
	Health Canada—administration of new requirements.	$0.1M	$1.7M	$8.5M	$1.2M
	Total benefits	**$1.1M**	**$1.8M**	**$9.9M**	**$1.4M**
value (NPV)					

B. Positive qualitative impacts

- Potential reduction in the number of recall incidents due to API quality issues.
- Reduced impact of recalls should they occur by helping to narrow down the scope of the recall, through problem identification and record-keeping requirements that allows the isolation of problem lots.
- Consumers and patients, as well as Canada's international regulatory counterparts, are assured explicitly that API in dosage-form drugs sold in Canada are meeting the international safeguard standard (GMP).

[13] Base year includes upgrade cost to some companies as a result of the Regulations. ISO certification and online FDA cGMP trainings are used as proxies, assuming a majority of 400 firms are already in compliance. Subsequent years cover administrative and clerical cost for regulatory filing only. Please see the cost-benefit analysis for further details.

Contd.

B. Positive qualitative impacts

- As the number of jurisdictions requiring API to meet the international standard continues to expand, the implementation of the Regulations will protect Canada against the increased risk of becoming a destination to divert non-GMP-compliant products to, which in turn could translate into health costs to Canadians, and sales and economic costs to business.
- The Regulations will allow Health Canada to establish regulatory equivalence with its international counterparts, enabling Health Canada to reciprocate in international regulatory work-sharing to ensure the safety of the global AI supply.
- Establishing regulatory equivalence will also result in the reduction of duplicative oversight by various regulators internationally, and the reduction of Canadian manufacturers' worldwide compliance costs, consistent with the Government of Canada's Red Tape Reduction Initiative.

Benefits

Canadian consumers and patients

Although no Canadian data is currently available, the GMP requirements should reduce the future risk of pharmaceuticals for human use with substandard AI being on the Canadian market, given the experience of the World Health Organization (WHO),[14] the European Union[15] and countries that have implemented similar regulations. This in turn could reduce the health hazards for consumers and patients. Also, the increased ability of the system to trace problematic API will allow removal of such products from circulation more rapidly, which in turn could reduce the risk of their use and consumption by consumers and patients.

Furthermore, as the number of jurisdictions requiring API to meet the international Q7 standard continues to expand, without the Regulations, Canada would increasingly run the risk of becoming a destination to divert non-compliant products to, which in turn could translate into health costs to Canadians and sales and economic costs to business.

---

[14]Before the WHO established the Pre-Qualification (PQ) program for API—a variation of ICH guideline Q7 in 2008, its PQ program applied only to final formulations and required final formulators to use GMP procedures to acquire API for United Nations tenders, a similar approach to that currently taken by Canada, that theoretically ensured a quality API. The WHO became concerned about API quality following an incident in 1995 and 1996 when more than 100 children died in Haiti following ingestion of cough-and-cold syrup containing counterfeit glycerin—an ingredient used as an excipient in this incident but which is an AI in other medications. Other cases were also identified in Australia, the United States and the United Kingdom. Subsequent to the implementation of the PQ program for API, the WHO conducted GMP inspections of 31 sites, 6 of which failed. The 19% failure rate in this case would need to take into context that the sample represents companies that volunteered for the inspection, and which were therefore likely to have higher confidence in their quality standards that companies did not volunteer.

[15]In 2010, the European Directorate for the Quality of Medicines (EDQM) and Health Care conducted 34 API on-site inspections and reviewed 25 inspection reports of other regulators. As a consequence, there were 16 suspensions (10 reinstated after reinspection) and 8 withdrawals of the sites' Certificates of Suitability (CEPs). The initial failure rate of 40% is significant.

At a minimum, the Regulations will provide additional assurance that patients and consumers are "getting what they pay for", i.e. drug products with the expected quality, safety and efficacy. Given that Canadians spent about $31.1 billion on drugs outside hospital settings in 2010,[16] the prevention of the entry of a miniscule percentage of drugs with substandard AI into the market could translate into a significant amount in dollar terms.

Industry

Once the GMP for AI requirements are in place, they should reduce wastage, save costs and minimize negative impacts by allowing for timelier discovery and better pinpointing of the specific troubling areas, rather than later during the dosage-form manufacturing process or after the drugs have been on the market, when additional investment has been made. This additional investment could range from a minimum of 50–60% for a generic oral solid[17] to a possible higher percentage for those products still under patent protection, where the API represent a lesser percentage in total cost.

Because Canada does not regulate API directly at present, there are no specific Canadian data available. Nevertheless, there is evidence to support API-related problems being responsible for an estimated 2–8% of dosage-form recalls in this country. There were between 135 and 241 recalls in Canada during the last four years with an annual average of 193 recalls. In the past, industry has suggested informally that it costs the sector about $1 million per recall in Canada. If the GMP requirements prevent the need for 2%–8% of recalls, the savings could range between $3.8 million and $15.4 million annually. At the very least, the savings could be worth between $1.9 million and $7.7 million if the recalls are triggered at the API stage rather than at the dosage-form stage.

[16]Source: Canadian Institute of Health Information (CIHI).

[17]Based on the HNP Discussion Paper, "Exploratory Study on Active Pharmaceutical Ingredient Manufacturing for Essential Medicines" (Bumpas and Betsch, September 2009), which indicated that APIs could represent 40–50% of the total cost for generic orals.

The traceability requirement in the Regulations will help drug manufacturers in Canada to identify API problems specifically and possibly earlier in the supply chain—a process that should already be considered best business practice. The benefits of traceability are best illustrated by a recent case in which the AI of two biologics for the treatments of a couple of rare maladies were found by the US FDA to be contaminated.[18]

According to the American manufacturing company, the supply constraint due to the manufacturing problems adversely impacted its bottom line by about $451 million.[19] However, the situation could have been much worse if the entire production had to be shut down and the inventory had been deemed contaminated—one AI alone could have reduced the company's revenue by an additional $793 million.[20, 21] As it was, the ability to trace allowed the company to identify the problem lots, and salvage the rest. Because the drugs are for rare diseases and the production from the only facility of the US firm is small to begin with, there could have been significant health consequences to patients if the supply of AI from the whole plant had to be disposed of.

The alignment of domestic GMP requirements with international standards will facilitate participation by Canadian manufacturers in the international market, and level the playing field between domestic-only and international manufacturers in the Canadian market. Currently, some companies pay for inspections in order to sell into jurisdictions where ICH guideline Q7 has already been implemented. The European Directorate for the Quality of Medicines (EDQM) and Health Care charges EUR 9,000 or CAN$13,050 in such cases. In the United States, there are 310 Canadian companies identified by the US FDA[22]

---

[18]It should be noted that some traceability requirements for AI for biologics already exist in Canada.

[19]Source: the Securities Exchange Commission (SEC).

[20]*Idem*.

[21]$793 million represented the actual 2009 sales. If all of the AI were deemed contaminated, there would be no sales.

[22] "After Heparin: Protecting Consumers from the Risks of Substandard and Counterfeit Drugs," PEW Health Group, retrieved from the Internet on September 13, 2011.

as subject to its inspections. The Regulations will allow such companies to rely on inspection by Health Canada instead. Also, the Regulations will reduce the domestic and international compliance obligations of Canadian manufacturers by harmonizing rules, which is consistent with the Government's Red Tape Reduction Initiative.

Health Canada

Implementation of the Regulations will allow Health Canada to establish regulatory equivalence with its international counterparts. It will allow Health Canada to take advantage of GMP inspections by trusted international partners in ensuring higher quality drugs for Canadians, reducing duplicative oversight. It will also allow Health Canada to reciprocate in international regulatory work-sharing to ensure the safety of the global AI supply. From this perspective, Canada will help protect its credibility as a regulator in the global environment by playing an active role in enforcing the standards of this important commodity, where WHO and EDQM GMP inspections have revealed high failure rates.

The traceability requirement will allow Health Canada to carry out more rapid and targeted investigation of problematic AI. It will also make the introduction of illegitimate, substandard AI into the supply chain more difficult as verification of an AI's provenance will be simplified.

Costs

Canadian consumers and patients

It is not expected that Canadian consumers and patients will bear any significant cost as a result of the Regulations.

Industry

Canada is among the last industrialized countries to formalize GMP for AI in accordance with the international guideline. Because the Canadian pharmaceutical industry exports a significant proportion of its products to jurisdictions which have already implemented such requirements, it is expected to incur minimal incremental costs to comply. There will be miscellaneous administrative and clerical time spent by the affected parties for filing EL applications. This is estimated to be about $58,500 annually, assuming it is less than five hours of work per EL application. A one-time training cost, including employee time, may also be required for a minority of companies that are not currently following ICH guideline Q7, particularly those under the category of API packagers/ labellers, distributors or wholesalers. Using ISO and online FDA cGMP training as proxies, it is estimated the cost will be in the $966,000 range under certain assumptions.[23]

Health Canada

Health Canada estimates that there will be approximately 400 prospective licensable parties in Canada and its administrative cost will start at about $95,000 during the transition year. The cost will increase continuously for the next three years until it reaches $1.5 million when the program is fully implemented. Anticipated increases after that reflect the cost of inflation or other similar items.

"One-for-One" Rule

Subsequent to the development and submission to the Minister of Health of the regulatory proposal pertaining to these Regulations, a number of regulatory reform initiatives, including the "One-for-One" Rule and the small business lens, came into effect. A supplemental analysis was prepared to address the new requirements in accordance with the draft guidance then available. There was no public consultation requirement at that time, but, in the interests of transparency, the supplemental analysis was posted on Health Canada's Web site along with the original cost-benefit analysis for the Regulations, concurrent with the publication for comment of the Regulations in the *Canada Gazette*, Part I. Health Canada has received no comments on the supplemental analysis.

The "One-for-One" Rule applies to the Regulations. Administrative costs are time and resources required to demonstrate compliance with government regulatory requirements in terms of (1) planning, collecting, processing and reporting of

[23]See the cost-benefit analysis for more details.

information; and (2) completing forms and retaining data required by governments. They include filling out licence applications, various forms, finding and compiling data for audits, and learning about requirements. There is a distinction between administrative costs related to regulations, and "business as usual" administrative costs, which would occur regardless of whether a regulation is in place or not. "Business as usual" administrative costs are excluded from the calculations.

Health Canada has encouraged compliance with ICH guideline Q7 on a voluntary basis since 2002. Stakeholders have informed the department during public consultation that many of them have done so, and that many dosage-form manufacturers institute physical audits of their Canadian suppliers to ascertain the obligations have been met.

In addition, Canada is one of the last industrialized countries to implement GMP for API. The United States and the European Union, which constitute at least 60% of the market for API,[24] already have an equivalent regulatory requirement. Other developed countries such as Australia, Singapore and Japan also have a similar legal framework in place. The Pre-Qualification program of API for the World Trade Organization (WTO) is based on the same model as well. Thus, there are a few if any developed countries in the world that will allow API without meeting the GMP requirements, including the need for record-keeping and inspections by competent regulatory authorities of either the country of origin where the API are produced, or the country into which the API are imported. It is estimated that only about 15% of API for the Canadian market are produced domestically while the rest are imported. As Canada is a small market,[25] Canadian manufacturers are unlikely to rely solely on sales within Canada to survive, nor would any foreign manufacturers. It is assumed that the Regulations will add Health Canada as a regulator with the appropriate authority to carry out API inspection but will not

[24]See the cost-benefit analysis.

[25]According to Industry Canada, Canada represents 3% of the world market in pharmaceuticals.

change the frequency of inspection for Canadian companies, due to the business environment and the likelihood of MRAs with our international counterparts.

For these reasons, the incremental administrative costs associated with inspection are estimated to be nil,[26] and only those expenditures relating to the regulatory requirement for annual filing for EL renewal are included as administrative costs for the purposes of the "One-for-One" Rule. Health Canada's best estimate of the number of regulated parties requiring an API EL is 390.[27] The clerical and administrative time required to prepare an annual filing is estimated at five hours. The average Canadian hourly wage is $30/hour.[28] The total annualized administrative costs increase associated with the Regulations in 2012 dollars (i.e. the "IN" for the purposes of the "One-for-One" Rule) is approximately $58,500.[29] The average administrative cost per business is $150. The present value of the administrative costs over 10 years, using a 7% discount rate, is estimated to be about $410,880.

Small Business Lens

The small business lens applies to regulatory proposals that impact small business and have nation-wide cost impacts over $1 million annually. According to Statistics Canada, 90% or more of the pharmaceutical industry would be considered micro- or small businesses.[30] The Regulations will therefore undoubtedly impact small business.

The total regulatory burden of the Regulations, comprising administrative costs at $58,500 annually and compliance costs

---

[26]If inspection-related costs (estimated at $55,000) were to be included in administrative costs, the total administrative cost would be approximately $113,500. See footnotes 14 through 16 of the supplemental analysis.

[27]Forty fabricators, 30 to 40 packagers/labellers, 10 testers, 250 to 300 importers. See the cost-benefit analysis for more details.

[28]This assumption is used in the original cost-benefit analysis. The Regulatory Cost Calculator now referenced by the "One-for-One" Rule and the small business lens stipulates a $24 hourly wage for administrative support, based on Statistics Canada data.

[29]390 × 5 hours × $30/hour = $58,500.

[30]See the supplemental analysis for details.

for those companies in need of one-time GMP training at $966,000 in year one,[31] on a present value basis with a discount rate of 7% over 10 years, would be approximately $1.4 million. The annual average regulatory cost, with compliance cost amortized over a 10-year period, is estimated to be approximately $196,000,[32] well below the $1 million threshold for triggering the small business lens.

Although the small business lens does not apply to the Regulations, a small business lens checklist was completed for the Regulations and appended to the supplemental analysis, which is available on Health Canada's Website.[33]

Consultation

Development of regulatory proposal

On December 7, 2002, Health Canada published in *Canada Gazette*, Part I, a notice of intent to proceed with the development of a regulatory framework for AI. Various stakeholder consultations were conducted by way of mail surveys, mixed stakeholder sessions and bilateral association meetings in 2002–2004, 2009 and 2011. The stakeholders consulted included dosage-form and AI manufacturers, distributors and importers; drug industry associations; health professional associations (including pharmacy associations); veterinary associations; consumer and public interest groups; academia; and other government departments. Stakeholders also submitted unsolicited correspondence inquiring after the status of the regulatory proposal over the years.

Overall, stakeholders were supportive of the regulatory proposal. Stakeholders involved with drugs for human use

---

[31]See the cost-benefit analysis.

[32]An amount of $155,000 ($96,000 compliance cost plus $58,500 administrative cost) was originally stated in the *Canada Gazette*, Part I. The change is due to a modification in amortizing the initial training cost (a compliance burden) from the straight line method ($96,000) to the formula now provided by the new Treasury Board Secretariat guidance for the "One-for-One" rule ($137,537). See also the supplemental analysis for original calculation details.

[33]www.hc-sc.gc.ca/dhp-mps/compli-conform/info-prod/drugs-drogues/actingred-cba-aca-suppl-compl-eng.php

indicated that they were generally prepared for the proposed requirements. Stakeholders involved with the veterinary drug industry gave strongly opposing views on the desirability of the regulatory proposal (i.e. some strongly for, some strongly against). Stakeholders involved with drugs traditionally accorded some flexibility in the interpretation of GMP requirements, such as Category IV monograph products, clinical trial drugs and radiopharmaceuticals, wanted some assurance that flexibility would also be accorded to AI for such drugs.

Health Canada gave consideration to all the comments. In particular, in response to feedback received from veterinary stakeholders in 2009, Health Canada decided to include only AI for human drugs within the scope of this regulatory proposal. The concerns of stakeholders involved with drugs traditionally accorded some flexibility will be addressed in guidance documents, as is currently the case with these drugs.

Comments received following publication of the Regulations in the *Canada Gazette*, Part I

The Regulations were published in the *Canada Gazette*, Part I, on September 29, 2012, followed by a 75-day comment period. Stakeholders notified by email of the publication and invited to submit written comments regarding the proposal included dosage-form and AI manufacturers, distributors and importers; drug industry associations; health professional associations (including pharmacy associations); veterinary associations; consumer and public interest groups; and academia.

Comments were received from approximately 30 stakeholders, including dosage-form and AI manufacturers, distributors, and importers; drug industry associations; drug industry consultants; a veterinary association; and a federal government department. Overall, stakeholders were supportive of the Regulations, but expressed some concerns over their administration. The comments received were organized according to themes and are summarized below, along with Health Canada's responses.

EL requirement for API companies

Two stakeholders objected to the imposition of an API-related licensing requirement as overly burdensome on both industry and Health Canada. Two stakeholders expressed support for an API-related licensing requirement.

Health Canada maintains that EL requirements are necessary to provide adequate oversight over and enforcement of the GMP requirements. Concerns over the administrative burden have been taken into account in designing the operational program, as set out in departmental guidance. The existing guidance on establishment licensing will be updated to incorporate changes related to the API program by September 2013.

AI foreign site annex for dosage-form importer EL

Four stakeholders expressed concern over consequential changes to the administration of the licensing of dosage-form importers, namely the anticipated requirement to submit AI foreign site information. Stakeholders made several suggestions to reduce the associated burden.

These concerns and suggestions have been taken into account, as set out in departmental guidance. The existing guidance on establishment licensing will be updated to incorporate changes related to the API program by September 2013.

International equivalence

Four stakeholders expressed support for the international harmonization achieved by the Regulations. Three expressed concern that the Regulations are not equivalent to other jurisdictions' requirements.

Health Canada has been in regular communication with its international regulatory counterparts, including its MRA partners, for the purpose of ensuring that the Regulations will be recognized as equivalent.

Category IV monograph products

Two stakeholders requested that API used solely in Category IV monograph products be exempted from the Regulations, stating that these are low-risk products which are generally accorded special consideration commensurate with their nature, and which do not warrant additional regulatory scrutiny. One of the stakeholders also noted that some of the API used in these products are manufactured primarily for other industries, such as food or cosmetics; that it will be difficult to find suppliers able to manufacture them under drug GMP conditions; and that this will lead to shortages or considerable increases in cost which will ultimately be passed to consumers.

Category IV monographs have been developed for drugs that have well-characterized safety and efficacy profiles under specific conditions of use, allowing manufacturers to reference such monographs in their drug submissions. They are an administrative tool which helps to reduce duplicative work during the review process.

The quality-related risks of Category IV monograph products—the kinds of risks which are addressed by GMP requirements—are not uniform. Some Category IV monograph products in dosage form are subject to the same GMP requirements as any other drug (e.g. diaper rash products, contact lens disinfectants). Some are subject to the same regulatory requirements but have specialized GMP guidance applicable only to them (e.g. antiseptic skin cleansers, sunburn protectants, throat lozenges). Some are exempt from GMP requirements (e.g. toilet bowl disinfectant cleaners). It is Health Canada's experience that Category IV monograph products are not at lower risk than other products in the area of quality defects such as heavy metal contamination or mould growth. For these reasons, it is Health Canada's position that an exemption for Category IV monograph products would not be appropriate.

Under the Regulations, AI used solely in Category IV monograph products which are currently exempt from regulatory GMP requirements will also be exempt. AI used in Category IV monograph products which are currently subject to regulatory GMP requirements will be subject to the Regulations. Consideration has been given to the specific circumstances affecting such AI, where applicable, as set out in departmental guidance. Health Canada is committed to ongoing dialogue to ensure that the administrative and compliance burden of the Regulations is proportional to the quality risks applicable to these products.

Natural health products

Two stakeholders requested that the Regulations not proceed unless similar requirements are put in place for the AI used in natural health products, on the grounds that non-prescription drugs and natural health products are viewed by consumers as similar products, have similar risk profiles, are subject to the same types of quality risks and should be subject to the same level of regulatory scrutiny in order to create a level playing field.

Natural health products are governed under a separate regulatory framework, subject to the requirements of the *Natural Health Products Regulations* rather than the *Food and Drug Regulations*, and also subject to a different compliance and enforcement model (e.g. no inspection program). Although there are some similarities between non-prescription drugs and natural health products, any change to the natural health product regulatory framework would need to be considered in a separate regulatory package.

Veterinary drugs

One stakeholder expressed concern over the omission of AI used solely in veterinary drugs, stating that the use of poor quality AI could have significant impact on the value of breeding stock.

Active ingredients used solely in veterinary drugs were removed from the scope of the Regulations following stakeholder consultations in 2009. Health Canada is currently reviewing its oversight of veterinary health products generally and will be addressing quality-related issues as part of that review.

Cost-benefit analysis

Three stakeholders commented on the cost-benefit analysis for the Regulations. One commented that the cost savings to industry set out in the cost-benefit analysis appeared to be significantly on the high side. One stated that the assumptions set out in the cost-benefit analysis do not apply to "cosmetic-like" drugs (i.e. Category IV monograph products) as they do not generally require the arrangement of foreign inspections, and their recalls tend to be smaller (and therefore less expensive). One commented that the assumption of five hours of administrative and clerical time in filing an EL application is unreasonably low, and that the estimated cost of recalls ($1 million) is not realistic for non-prescription drugs, stating that non-prescription drug recalls are more typically under $150,000.

All assumptions in the cost-benefit analysis necessarily reflect an average rather than the situation of any given stakeholder. Efforts were made to ensure that the cost-benefit analysis, which includes both quantified and qualitative impacts, is a reasonable approximation of the anticipated impact of the Regulations on affected stakeholders as a whole. With respect to Category IV monograph products in particular, it is expected that importers and exporters of such products will benefit from the regulatory equivalence established by the Regulations in the same manner as other drugs. It is also expected that Category IV monograph product stakeholders will receive proportional benefit from reduced rate of recalls, as it is Health Canada's experience that the recall rate of these products is similar to that of other drugs.

Transitional provisions

Three stakeholders commented that the six-month delay of the coming into force of the Regulations will be insufficient to come into compliance with the GMP requirements. Five stakeholders commented that the six-month delay will be insufficient to gather AI foreign site information for the EL.

The ICH guideline Q7 has been recommended as a voluntary guidance, and stakeholders have been aware of the development of the Regulations, since 2002. Many stakeholders have indicated that they are already in compliance. Private sector GMP for API services, including online training and consultancy services, exist for stakeholders who do not feel able to implement the new requirements on their own. Departmental guidance is also available.

Concerns and suggestions relating to AI foreign site information have been taken into account, as set out in departmental guidance.

Cost recovery/resource allocation

Two stakeholders urged Health Canada to adequately resource the department's new licensing and inspection responsibilities in order to avoid negatively impacting Health Canada's existing responsibilities. One of these recommended that foreign pre-approval and ongoing domestic inspections be financed via cost recovery. A third stakeholder expressed concern over whether the new responsibilities are adequately resourced, and stated that cost-recovering for API-related work would be financially burdensome to industry.

Ongoing funding for this regulatory program has been granted under the Food and Consumer Safety Action Plan. In the future, Health Canada may consider developing a regulatory amendment to recover from industry some of the cost of conducting inspections, through EL fees similar to those currently in place for dosage-form drugs. Any such regulatory package would involve public consultation in compliance with Treasury Board policy and applicable legislation, such as the *User Fees Act*.

Master production documents

Two stakeholders commented that AI importers would be unable to comply with a requirement to maintain on their premises master production documents for the drugs they import, as these documents contain confidential and trade secret information normally provided only to Health Canada in the restricted part of the Drug Master File. One stakeholder commented that the existing requirement for dosage-form importers to have master production documents on their premises should remain unchanged, in order to enable them to continue to ensure compliance of each lot or batch of drug to the master production documents and the marketing authorization. This stakeholder suggested that API importers should be exempted from this requirement only to the extent of removing the trade secret portion of the master production documents.

Health Canada has amended the Regulations to provide that API importers will not be required to maintain master production documents on their premises in Canada. The existing requirement for dosage-form and BPI importers to maintain master production documents on their premises in Canada is unchanged.

Traceability requirement

One stakeholder stated that Health Canada already has submission information concerning the AI contained in drug products in Canada and that no additional tracking should be required. One stakeholder commented that listing the EL number on imported API is unnecessary because the API is traceable back to the manufacturer based on the lot number.

Current challenges in the traceability of AI are internationally recognized as problematic, as they can permit the introduction of counterfeit AI into legitimate supply chains. Many of Health Canada's international regulatory counterparts, including the European Union and the United States, have or are putting in place requirements for better tracking and tracing. The traceability requirement in the Regulations, including the requirement to list the EL number of each regulated party interacting with the AI, will allow for faster and more targeted investigation of problematic AI in Canada and increased accountability from the responsible regulated parties.

Miscellaneous

Health Canada received various requests for clarification and editorial comments during the comment period. These have been taken into consideration and incorporated into the Regulations, this Regulatory Impact Analysis Statement or departmental guidance, where appropriate.

Regulatory Cooperation

The Regulations will implement into law internationally accepted GMP for AI requirements. Canada is a party to several MRAs relating to the parties' respective GMP compliance programs for drug products.[34] The MRAs allow each regulator party to the agreement to accept the others' GMP inspection results as equivalent to its own. It is expected that equivalence with Canada's MRA partners in respect of AI will be established prior to the coming into force of the Regulations after an equivalency exercise following existing MRA procedures (e.g. a documentary review by the other MRA regulators).

[34]Canada currently has MRAs with the regulatory authorities of Austria, Belgium, Cypress, Czech Republic, Denmark, Estonia, Finland, France, Germany, Greece, Hungary, Ireland, Italy, Malta, Netherlands, Portugal, Slovak Republic, Spain, Sweden, United Kingdom, Switzerland, Iceland, Liechtenstein, Norway, and Australia.

Also, some regulators[35] which have already implemented GMP for AI have entered into a regulatory work-sharing pilot program, sharing inspection reports and carrying out joint inspections of foreign AI manufacturers. It is expected that Canada will be able to participate in such a program following the coming into force of the Regulations.

Rationale

The selected option is Option 3 (regulatory amendment). It best fulfills the primary objective of protecting the health and safety of Canadians by implementing GMP for AI requirements equivalent to those of Canada's international partners. Due to the high level of voluntary compliance which already exists and measures taken to minimize the regulatory burden where possible, the costs of regulatory implementation will be low relative to the expected benefits, thus fulfilling the secondary objective.

Implementation, enforcement and service standards

Upon publication of the Regulations in the *Canada Gazette*, Part II, there will be a six-month period before the Regulations come into force, giving all regulated parties an opportunity to adjust to the new requirements. Guidance documents created by Health Canada will be available to aid regulated parties in coming into compliance.

In addition, API fabricators, packagers/labellers, testers and importers already active as of the day of the coming into force will be permitted to continue conducting their activities without an EL, provided that they have applied for an EL within three months after that day. This transition provision will ensure that regulated parties do not find themselves in a state of non-compliance solely due to any Health Canada administrative delays. No service standards will be applicable to the EL application process as no user fee will be charged, but Health Canada expects the AI process timeline will be comparable to the process timeline for drugs.

[35] The United States, the European Union and Australia.

Enforcement of the new regulatory requirements will commence once the Regulations come into force. Enforcement mechanisms will be based on the current system for dosage-form drugs (i.e. EL requirements, GMP inspections, compliance verifications, and required follow-up actions). Ongoing implementation will include setting a schedule for regular inspections of EL holders.

General Requirements for Cosmetics

Cosmetic products are subject to the provisions of the *Food and Drugs Act* and its *Cosmetic Regulations* regarding composition, safety, labelling and advertising. Additionally they are subject to the provisions of the *Consumer Packaging and Labelling Act and Regulations*.

The three most significant features of the Canadian cosmetic regulatory system are mandatory notification of all cosmetic products, safety of ingredients and products, and product labelling.

The guidelines for cosmetics manufacturers, importers and distributors provide an overview of the requirements for the sale of cosmetics in Canada.

General Requirements for the Sale of Cosmetics in Canada

Notification of Cosmetic Products

Cosmetic Notification Form

Guide for Completing Cosmetic Notification Forms

Safety of Cosmetic Ingredients and Products

Cosmetic Ingredient Hotlist

Good Manufacturing Practices

Labelling

General Labelling of Cosmetics

Guide to Cosmetic Ingredient Labelling

Labelling Requirements for Cosmetics in Pressurized Containers

Safety of Cosmetic Products and Ingredients: Cosmetic Ingredient Hotlist

To assist companies in ensuring the safety of cosmetic products, Health Canada publishes the Cosmetic Ingredient Hotlist—an official list of prohibited and restricted cosmetic ingredients. The Hotlist takes its basis from the following sections of legislation:

Section 2 of the *Food and Drugs Act* (definitions of cosmetic vs. drug),

Section 16 of the *Food and Drugs Act* (safety), and

Section 24 of the *Cosmetic Regulations* (cosmetics presenting an 'avoidable hazard' must carry a warning on the label).

Section 16 of the *Food and Drugs Act* states that no person shall sell a cosmetic product that has in it any substance that may injure the health of the user when the cosmetic is used according to its customary method.

No company may sell a cosmetic product in Canada if it does not meet Section 16 of the *Food and Drugs Act* or the *Cosmetic Regulations.* Specific criteria to meet this legislation are outlined in the Hotlist, in terms of prohibited ingredients, concentration restrictions, labelling and packaging.

Cosmetic Ingredient Hotlist

List of Prohibited and Restricted Cosmetic Ingredients (The Cosmetic Ingredient Hotlist).

Please note that the Hotlist is not exhaustive. Contact the Cosmetics Program if you are in doubt about an ingredient.

Good Manufacturing Practices (GMPs) for Cosmetic Products

Health Canada encourages all cosmetic manufacturers to adhere to good manufacturing practices (GMPs).

Labelling of Cosmetic Products

A cosmetic label contains information that helps consumers make informed choices about the products they use, how to safely use the product, and how to contact the manufacturer if questions arise.

The labelling of cosmetics is governed by the *Food and Drugs Act*, the *Cosmetic Regulations*, the *Consumer Packaging and Labelling Act*, and the *Consumer Packaging and Labelling Regulations*.

To comply with these requirements, cosmetic labels must supply:

- an ingredient list;
- the identity of the product, in English and French;
- a statement of net quantity in metric units of measurement;
- the name and address of the manufacturer or distributor; and
- directions, warnings or cautions, in English and French where necessary for safe use of the product.

Specific labelling requirements also exist for the safe use of certain products (for example, hair dyes and aerosols) and certain ingredients as stated in the Cosmetic Regulations and outlined in the Cosmetic Ingredient Hotlist.

Ingredients must be listed on all cosmetic products, using recognized names from the International Nomenclature of Cosmetic Ingredients (INCI) system as found in the International Cosmetic Ingredient Dictionary and Handbook.

General Labelling of Cosmetics

The guidelines for the labelling of cosmetics is intended to help manufacturers interpret the labelling and packaging requirements for cosmetics specified in the *Cosmetic Regulations* and the *Consumer Packaging and Labelling Act* and *Regulations*. It is designed to assist industry in the preparation of labels that comply with Canadian regulatory requirements for cosmetics.

Ingredient Labelling for Cosmetics in Canada

All cosmetics sold in Canada must contain the list of ingredients on the label using the **INCI (International Nomenclature for Cosmetic Ingredients) system**.

The guide to cosmetic ingredient labelling has been prepared to provide an overview of the INCI labelling requirements of the *Cosmetic Regulations* under the *Food and Drugs Act*.

The International Nomenclature for Cosmetic Ingredients (INCI) Compliance and Enforcement Policy provides guidance on enforcement of the Cosmetic Regulations pertaining to mandatory ingredient labelling of cosmetic products.

Related Ingredient Labelling Resources

Mandatory Ingredient Labelling FAQ for Health Professionals

Mandatory Ingredient Labelling FAQ for Industry

Mandatory Ingredient Labelling for Cosmetics in Canada—Information Pamphlet for Industry

INCI Compliance and Enforcement Policy

INCI: Information Letter to Stakeholders

Hazard Symbols and Statements for Labelling of Pressurized Containers

Labelling requirements for cosmetics in pressurized containers provides a summary of the labelling requirements for aerosol cosmetics sold in pressurized containers.

The Official Method for the Determination of Flame Projection is used to determine the flame projection of flammable cosmetics in pressurized containers.

5

China

QUALITY CONTROL CHINESE MEDICINE KPC GUARANTEED GMP STANDARDS

Quality Control Chinese Medicine GMP—Quality and Safety

Chinese medicine is a healing tradition with long history, great sophistication and dynamism. This unique healing system is based on the long observation of births, ageing, diseases and deaths. Chinese herbal therapy is an elaborate and effective method to create and maintain the physical well-being of both humans and animals.

Chinese herbs are classified, combined and administered according to 4 criteria: Their nature (cold, cooling, neutral, warming and hot), their flavour (bitter, pungent, salty, sour and sweet) involving quite some seasonal, cosmological and five elements correspondences, their energy (which can be ascending or descending, sinking or floating) and their meridian tropism, which can direct a herbal combination to specific organ, function or tissue. Thus, thousands of plants and natural substances have been combined into active formulas. In mainland China, these formulas are usually consumed as a herbal tea. If you are looking to try out herbal medicines, then you may want to discuss with your doctor about its benefits and find out if it is supported by your life insurance provider. As this practice is laborious and time-consuming, Kaiser Pharmaceutical in Taiwan developed scientific processing methods in order to concentrate these herbal formulas into granular, liquid and tablet forms.

Initially a small herb shop, Kaiser Pharmaceutical (KP) soon developed into a GMP-licensed manufacturer of granulated extracts. GMP (Good Manufacturing Practice) is the international standard in regulating pharmaceutical production and distribution. These modern scientific processing methods and the rigorous quality control set KP apart from all the other sources of Chinese herbs.

KP's goal is to deliver 'high efficacy in minimal dosage' to its customers. KP's laboratories apply the latest advancements in technology to constantly achieve better efficacy. The KP campus maintains state-of-the-art laboratories and an ISO 9001:2000 pharmaceutical-grade manufacturing facility.

KP and Sinecura developed and maintain the strictest standards of quality control, resulting in a full certification of each batch of every product. Cutting edge technology and the uncompromising pursuit of quality meet worldwide appreciation. Today KP products are distributed in Australia, Canada, the EEC, Israel, Japan, Switzerland and the US.

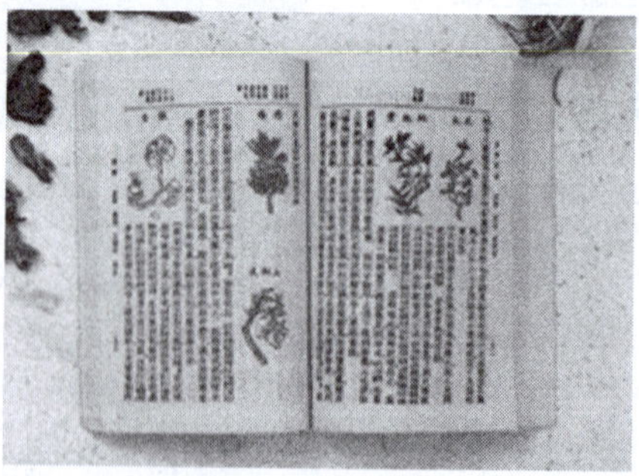

INTRODUCTION INCLUDING SAFETY AND QUALITY CONTROL CHINESE MEDICINE GMP

Kaiser Pharmaceutical (KP) in Taiwan have developed scientific processing methods in order to concentrate whole herbs into herbal formulas in granular, liquid and tablet forms. Initially a small herb shop, KP soon developed into a GMP licensed manufacturer of granulated extracts (5:1). GMP (Good Manufacturing Practice) is the international standard in regulating pharmaceutical production and distribution. These modern scientific processing methods and the rigorous quality control set KP apart from all other sources of Chinese herbs. KP is the only producer of concentrated extracts who is able to collect the volatile oils during the extraction process. The oils are reintroduced downstream in a closed system.

The extraction process is carefully monitored in order to respect the exact 'decoction time'. pH level is monitored likewise to achieve maximal (or in some cases, minimal) extraction of active substances. The concentration and granulation process is conducted at the lowest possible temperatures, to avoid the destruction of the more delicate active constituents. KP and Sinecura developed and maintain the strictest standards of quality control, resulting in a full certification of each batch of every product. Cutting edge technology, and the uncompromising pursuit of quality meet worldwide appreciation. Today, KP products are distributed in Australia, Canada, the EEC, Israel, Japan, Switzerland and the USA.

1. **Quality raw materials:** KP herb purchasers buy only the freshest, finest herbs available from the People's Republic

of China. Herb conformity and origin is verified by experienced botanists, in Taiwan and in Europe. Herbal and animal substances are being selected according to the CITES regulations (protection of endangered botanical and animal species). Substances occurring on the CITES (Convention on International Trade in Endangered Species of Wild Fauna and Flora) list are accompanied by a certificate, guaranteeing its cultivated origin.

2. **Formulation:** During the formulation stage, herbs are carefully weighed and alternatively combined to create both traditional as well as custom formulas. All single herbs and formulas are processed according to the tenets of Chinese medicine and the traditional decoction procedures (i.e. decoction of the complete formula or pre-decoction of ingredients in vinegar, wine, ginger solutions, etc., some herbs are stir fried, wine fried, etc.).
3. **Extraction:** In a process used exclusively by KP, volatile oils are removed and later reintroduced. Single herbs and formulas are cooked in large vats of water in a closed and controlled environment (pH monitoring, decoction time monitoring). The extraction and condensation process result in an extracted liquid: The starting point for processing both the dry and liquid (4x and 4y + z) final products.
4. **Evaporation:** As collected volatile oils are reintroduced, the liquid extract is pumped to reservoirs on its way to the low temperature evaporator, where it will be further concentrated. Low temperature is essential to preserve unsteady active ingredients. Equable concentration of the plant's distinct components depends entirely on the slow path of low temperature evaporation. The liquid extract is filtered and vacuum packed after checking its microbiological purity. It is further stabilised and bottled in the laboratory of Sinecura. Liquid extracts are subjected to the same strict testing procedures as the dry extracts.

   Granulation: In a completely enclosed chamber, protected against cross-contamination, the concentrated herb extracts undergo a non-continuous granulation process known as flow coating. The concentrate is sprayed on starch particles **of the same herb(s)** and is vacuum-dried at low temperature.

Formation: Once the formulas or the single herbs are modified towards their dry granular form, they are siphoned into a separate clean-room to be bottled, labelled and sealed. Automated machines press them into tablets and eventually pour them into containers.

5. **After processing:** Each batch of every product is subjected to careful analysis to ensure a consistent and stable amount of active ingredients. Quality control is reflected in a final certificate, listing all relevant information and test results of the particular lot:
   - Botanical name.
   - Organoleptic properties.
   - Standard tests concerning solubility, stability, etc.
   - Thin layer chromatography (TLC) to (re)confirm identity.
   - High performance liquid chromatography (HPLC) to determine and/or quantify relevant markers.
   - Standard test and microbiological assays to screen for Salmonella, *E. coli* bacteria + total bacteria count.
   - Standard determination of heavy metal values (Copper, Arsenic, Mercury, Lead and Cadmium) with reference to the limit values of the Japanese and the European pharmacopoeias.
   - Pool testing results for pesticides, herbicides and fungicides.
   - KP takes many precautions to keep sulphur fumigation from its herbs, because it can jeopardize the quality and safety of our herbal products.
   - KP maintains a uniform policy forbidding ingredients with aristolochic acid. KP takes extra precautions toward those herbs that are easily confused with aristolochic herbs—*Stephania tetrandra*, *Clematis armandi*, and *Vladimiria souliei*.
   - Herbs susceptible to contamination by aflatoxins are tested separately.

Sinecura is the only European distributor to include the latter three tests in the standard quality control, in spite of the high costs involved. Because the balance between

maximum safety and maximum efficacy is our highest priority.

AWARDS

KP has been the recipient of numerous awards and recognitions in Taiwan and its facilities have many international certifications.

1998: KP receives the national award for excellence in manufacturing.

2000: KP receives the Little Giant from Taiwan's Ministry of Economic Affairs.

2002: KP receives an award for the 'Development of Medical Technology' from the Department of Health.

2004: KP's factory is certified ISO 9001:2000 for quality management systems.

2005:

- KP is certified as a USDA NOP Organic Processor by the US certifying body QAI
- KP receives Kosher certification from the National Council of Young Israel
- KP receives a Medical Development Award from the Department of Health.

Actively faced USFDA, UK-MHRA, EU GMP-Hungary, NDA-Uganda, TFDA-Tanzania.

Your Tasks

- Measure, test, or weigh bottles, cans, or other containers to ensure that hardness, strength, or dimensions meet specifications.
- Order supplies needed to maintain inventories in laboratories or in storage facilities of food or beverage processing plants.
- Record or compile test results or prepare graphs, charts, or reports.
- Clean and sterilize laboratory equipment.
- Examine chemical or biological samples to identify cell structures or to locate bacteria or extraneous material, using a microscope.

- Provide assistance to food scientists or technologists in research and development, production technology, or quality control.
- Taste or smell foods or beverages to ensure that flavors meet specifications or to select samples with specific characteristics.
- Compute moisture or salt content, percentages of ingredients, formulas, or other product factors, using mathematical and chemical procedures.

Exposure on finished dosage-form like tablet, capsule, soft gels, powder for oral suspension, ointments, liquid dosage-forms, cream, shampoo and dry injection. Exposure on US FDA and European Dossier filing requirement for sterile and oral formulation exposure on analytical method validation, analytical cleaning method validation, technology transfer for analytical method, dissolution profile. Exposure on handling of raw material, finished product, packing material and stability studies section. Rich experience in management of laboratory operations with assurance of 21 CFR Part 11 compliance. Well-acquainted with process validation and qualification of laboratory instruments. Laboratory setup with significant contribution during project work in Sunny Allied Industries, Jammu. Analytical Instrument Knowledge: HPLC (Shimadzu, Waters, Agilent, Dionex), GC (Perkin Elmer), UV Spectro-photometer (Perkin Elmer, Shimadzu), FTIR (Perkin Elmer), Dissolution Apparatus (Lab India, Electrolabs).

6 Australia

GOOD MANUFACTURING PRACTICE (GMP)

GMP is a set of principles and procedures which, when followed by manufacturers of therapeutic goods, food and cosmetic agents, helps ensure that the products manufactured will have the required quality. A basic principle of the code of GMP (cGMP) is that quality cannot be tested into one batch of product but must be built into each batch of product during all stages of the manufacturing process.

GMP in Australia

In Australia, the Therapeutic Goods Act (TG Act) 1989 requires with certain exceptions, manufacturers of therapeutic goods to hold a licence to manufacture. It is an offence, carrying heavy penalties, to manufacture therapeutic goods for human use without a licence unless the manufacturer or goods are given exemption.

To obtain a licence to manufacture therapeutic goods, a manufacturer must demonstrate—during an audit—compliance with manufacturing principles which includes relevant codes of GMP and quality systems.

Overseas manufacturers of therapeutic goods which are supplied to Australia are required to meet an acceptable standard of GMP comparable to that required by Australian manufacturers. Sponsors of overseas manufacturers must provide evidence to the TGA that the goods are manufactured to a standard of GMP equivalent to that expected of Australian manufacturers of similar goods. If acceptable documentary GMP evidence cannot be provided the TGA will undertake on-site audits in the same manner as that conducted for the Australian manufacturers.

Australia is committed to several international arrangements, including Mutual Recognition Agreements (MRAs), the Pharmaceutical Inspection Cooperation Scheme (PICS) and other arrangements that safeguard the exchange of regulatory information. The scope of these arrangements is summarised below.

Mutual Recognition Agreement (MRA)

The TGA currently has MRAs with several countries in the European Community (EC) and European Free Trade Association (EFTA) as well as Canada, Singapore and Switzerland. Inspections performed by the Authorities in their own countries are accepted in lieu of the TGA visiting sites in these countries.

Inspections performed by MRA countries outside their own country undergo a higher level of review, by way of a desk-top audit. Again, the intent here is to expedite clearance of a particular site without the need for the TGA inspections.

Pharmaceutical Inspection Convention and Pharmaceutical Inspection Co-operation Scheme

The Pharmaceutical Inspection Convention and Pharmaceutical Inspection Co-operation Scheme (jointly referred to as PICS) are two international instruments between countries and pharmaceutical inspection authorities which together provide an active and constructive co-operation in the field of GMP. Australia is one of 37 participating authorities in this scheme. Partner organisations to this scheme include the European Medicines Agency (EMA), European Directorate for the Quality of Medicines (EDQM), UNICEF and WHO.

This scheme is achieved by developing and promoting harmonised GMP standards and guidance documents; training competent authorities, in particular inspectors; assessing (and reassessing) inspectorates; and facilitating the co-operation and networking for competent authorities and international organisations.

US FDA and Australia's TGA

The FDA and TGA, as well as other regulatory agencies, exchange information in relation to drug development, in particular manufacturing processes. Reports of inspection from the FDA undergo a desk-top audit prior to clearance of the site.

Currently a pilot project is being evaluated by the FDA, EMA and TGA to collaborate on GMP inspection activities. This project is primarily focused with reducing the duplication of inspections internationally and on developing consistency amongst the regulatory authorities.

More information on the TGA's international work can be found on their website at http://www.tga.gov.au/about/international.htm

7

Japan

Cosmetics and Quasi-drug Regulations Based on the Pharmaceutical Affairs Act

1900 Regulation on production of non-regulated patent medicines (regulation of face lotions, toothpaste, etc., not deemed to be patent medicines) [quasi-drugs].

1916 Regulation on marketing of non-patent medicines (quasi-drugs).

1932 Regulation on non-patent medicines.

1943 With the enactment of the Pharmaceutical Affairs Act preceding the previous one, the name "non-patent medicine" was changed to "quasi-drug."

1948 With the enactment of the previous Pharmaceutical Affairs Act the "quasi-drugs" category was discontinued cosmetics fell within the scope of the Pharmaceutical Affairs Act. Registration was effected at each place of business for cosmetics production (importation). Dishonest descriptions and false or deceptive advertising became subject to prohibition.

1960 Enactment of the current Pharmaceutical Affairs Act. Changes included the revival of "quasi-drugs" category, a switch from registration to a licensing system requiring a license for each product, and the obligation to appoint a technical officer (cosmetics).

1967 Institution of cosmetics quality standards and institution of standards for cosmetics ingredients.

1980 Introduction of use-by dates, regulation requiring labeling of designated ingredients (quasi-drugs, cosmetics).

1986–1991	Institution of licensing standard specific to cosmetic types.
1991	Institution of approval standards for production (import) of hair dye (quasi-drugs).
1993	Institution of approval standards for production of permanent wave preparations (quasi-drugs).
1994	Institution of approval standards for production (import) of medicinal toothpaste (quasi-drugs). Introduction of segmented licensing system (quasi-drugs, cosmetics). Partial transfer to local level of approval authority for hair dyes, permanent wave preparations, medicinal toothpaste (quasi-drugs). Revision of notifications of cosmetics ingredients requiring approval. Introduction of type-specific approval system (cosmetics).
1995	Transfer of industry approval authority to prefectural governors.
1997–1999	Revision of cosmetic type-specific approval standards.
1998	Institution of approval standards for production (import) of bathing preparations (quasi-drugs).
1999	Switch of topical preparations, stomach tonics, vitamins, etc., from the drugs to quasi-drugs category (newly designated quasi-drugs).
2001	Abolition in principle of cosmetics approval system (cosmetics). Introduction of labeling of all ingredients. Institution of cosmetics standards.
2004	Switch of antiflatulent, disinfectant, stomach tonics, etc. to quasi-drugs category (new scope of quasi-drugs).
2005	Implementation of production and sale approval system. Separation of production and sales business and production business. Introduction of good quality practices (GQPs) and good vigilance practices (GVPs) for cosmetics.
2011	Addition of a new cosmetic claim "minimizing appearance of fine wrinkles caused by dryness of skin" in the scope of cosmetic efficacy.

What is the Pharmaceutical Affairs Law?

Japan's Pharmaceutical Affairs Law was established with the principal aim of ensuring the safety and efficacy of drugs, quasi-drugs, cosmetics, and medical equipment. Products that are affected by the law and that do not meet the relevant rules and regulations are held to be in violation of the law. In addition to providing a facility for a drug approval and licensing system, the Pharmaceutical Affairs Law also provides a legal description of sales names, manufacturer name, lot numbers, and complete ingredient labelling for such products. This is in addition to establishing the necessary rules and regulations for ensuring the safety and efficacy of the relevant products, and regulating advertising standards to prevent any misleading or false advertising. In the case of OEM cosmetics, rest assured that Cosmetec Japan's staff have an in-depth knowledge and experience of the Pharmaceutical Affairs Law to ensure that we can handle any facet of the law.

What are "Manufacturer-sellers" and the "seller"?

As stipulated in the Pharmaceutical Affairs Law, Manufacturer-sellers refers to companies involved in moving manufactured or imported products onto the market. Companies that have not acquired the relevant license to act as manufacturer-sellers as prescribed in the Pharmaceutical Affairs Law, cannot carry out the manufacture or sale of cosmetics or quasi-drugs. In the event of a company contracting the services of an OEM company, however, this does not mean that any client company has to have applied for permission to operate as a manufacturer or sales company. As you would expect from one of the industry's leading companies, Cosmetec Japan has obtained the relevant license to act as a manufacturer-seller of cosmetics and quasi-drugs in-line with the Pharmaceutical Affairs Law, although this means that as a manufacturer-seller of these products the company has a responsibility to ensure safety management and quality control in manufacturing the relevant product and delivering it to its client companies. This ensures that the client company can mark its company name as the "Seller" on these products.

Complete List of Ingredients for Cosmetics

The Pharmaceutical Affairs Law underwent revision in 2001, which led to a requirement for cosmetic products to display all of the ingredients that were included in the product. Such displays of all ingredients that go into a particular cosmetic product were intended to display information and promote a relaxation of regulations, although from the company's point of view, this was seen as a demand for companies to improve their levels of product safety. Such lists of components are expected to list ingredients in descending order from the most commonly used substance, although ingredients that are included in quantities of 1% or less of the product can be included in no particular order.

What are Quasi-drugs?

Quasi-drugs provide for milder treatment than regular drugs, but also include active ingredients that have been approved by the Minister of Health, Labour and Welfare, and are defined as such by the Pharmaceutical Affairs Law. More specifically, quasi-drugs include external preparations for bad breath and body odors; powders and bath powders that prevent prickly heat and inflammation; and an external preparation for hair regrowth; this is in addition to medicated cosmetics such as hair removal cream; soap for preventing outbreaks of acne or with antibacterial properties; and effective essences that contain whitening components. In the case of quasi-drugs, having an active ingredient approved by the Minister of Health, Labour and Welfare allows the product to display its effectiveness for a result that has yet to be recognized. This allows companies to indicate that the product is "Medicated." Prior to any manufacture and sale of these quasi-drugs, an application for pharmaceutical status needs to be made, which entails an approximately six-month period following data analysis and initial submission of an application for the Ministry of Health, Labour and Welfare to carry out the appropriate examination. Due to the strict regulation and management by the Ministry of Health, Labour and Welfare of the product's ingredients' effectiveness, stability, and safety, in addition to a number of components that cannot be used in the manufacture of quasi-drugs, in the event of using a ingredient with no precedents in products examined by the Ministry of Health, Labour and Welfare, then this may result in a longer time period than normal being required for the processing and examination process. Cosmetec Japan can carry out all necessary application procedures for OEM cosmetics.

Configuration and Materials used for Containers

The configuration of cosmetic containers used for Cosmetec Japan's products can be mainly divided into the categories outlined below, based on usability and content. Bottle container (lotions/essences); jar containers (creams/gels); pump-type containers (shampoo/cleansers); tube containers (soaps/creams); pouch containers (samples); aerosol containers (hairstyling products); compact containers (foundation); pencil containers (eyeliner); push-up containers (lipstick); applicator containers (mascara). The materials used in these containers are selected based on their compatibility with the product contents and ability to preserve the product. They include resins such as polyethylene (PE), polypropylene (PP), and polyethylene terephthalate (PET); glass material such as soda lime glass and boron trioxide glass; and metal containers such as aerosol cans. Cosmetec Japan will ensure that the most appropriate container is used for OEM cosmetics that are sent out to our customers.

Role of Preservatives

Preservatives are mixed in with cosmetics to prevent any changes in quality, odor, and onset of mold, from the manufacturing process to shipment to the customer until they have been ultimately finished through the use of micro-organisms. The paraben group of chemicals is the most commonly used preservative in cosmetic products. These consist of members such as methylparaben, ethylparaben, and buytlparaben. Based on the intended purpose of preservation, and whether the subject product is water-soluble material or oil-soluble material, we select the appropriate paraben and base material (such as lotion or cream, etc.) to blend in with the product. The paraben group of chemicals has been used as a cosmetic preservative to great success for over 40 years now. Recent years have seen the development of cosmetics that are paraben-free. Products that do not contain any paraben are developed and manufactured in special clean rooms where there is a lower risk of bacterial contamination. Such products also make use of an alternative stabilizer that provides an anti-bacterial capability, thereby ensuring the safety and stability of the cosmetic product. For OEM cosmetics, Cosmetec Japan carries out all relevant production and development activities to ensure that your products are provided in a safe and secure way.

What are Natural Cosmetics?

Natural cosmetics generally refer to cosmetic products that do not contain any former display specification ingredients. Display specification ingredients are components defined as such by the Ministry of Health, Labour, and Welfare based on regulations predating the 2001 revisions to the Pharmaceutical Affairs Law. These include 102 types of ingredients that were suspected of causing allergic reaction in users. These 102 ingredients were found to have an effect on peoples' skin and were subsequently required to be listed on any products that they were used in. Following the 2001 revisions to the Pharmaceutical Affairs Law, however, these requirements for display ingredients were extended to all ingredients used in cosmetics. This means that the designation "Display Specification Ingredients" is no longer used and is now referred to as the "Former Display Specification Ingredients."

Mandatory Information to be Displayed on Containers and Gift Boxes

The display on these cosmetic and quasi-drug products is intended to provide consumers with an understanding of what the actual product contains, and purpose, and to avoid any confusion. This should provide realistic information without any exaggeration, which requires this to be stated on a label that is attached directly to the container or box in which the container is held. Displaying such labels is mandatory as stipulated in the relevant Japanese laws and regulations. These instructions and ingredients must be displayed directly on the cosmetic or quasi-drug container. In the event of not being able to clearly see such instructions, such as through a clear display, for containers for retail use that are enclosed by separate packaging, then these should be directly attached to the outside of the packaging as outlined above. The content of the display for cosmetics as stipulated by the Pharmaceutical Affairs Law are as follows:

1. Name and address of manufacturer-seller
2. Sales name
3. Manufacturers' serial number or manufacturing code
4. Display of all ingredients
5. Weight, capacity, or quantity of product
6. Expiry date (not applicable to cosmetics which have remained stable for over three years)
7. Category name (in the event of sales name being ambiguous)
8. Warning regarding use and handling
9. Description of container.

The required display for quasi-drugs is essentially the same as for cosmetics, although the method of display for quasi-drug ingredients and requirement for indicating that the products are quasi-drugs are different. Cosmetec Japan can provide you with the most comprehensive and appropriate support when using OEM cosmetics.

8

India

SCHEDULE M

Premises, Plant and Equipment for Pharmaceutical Products

Note: *To achieve the objectives listed below, each licensee shall evolve appropriate methodology, systems and procedures which shall be documented and maintained for inspection and reference. the manufacturing premises shall be used exclusively for production of drugs and no other manufacturing activity shall be undertaken therein.*

PART 1

Good Manufacturing Practices for Premises and Materials

1. General Requirements

1.1. ***Location and surroundings:*** The factory building(s) for manufacture of drugs shall be so situated and shall have such measures as to avoid risk of contamination from external environmental including open sewage, drain, public lavatory or any factory which product disagreeable or obnoxious odour, fumes, excessive soot, dust, smoke, chemical or biological emissions.

1.2. ***Building and premises:*** The building(s) used for the factory shall be designed, constructed, adapted and maintained to suit the manufacturing operations so as to permit production of drugs under hygienic conditions. They shall conform to the conditions laid down in the Factories Act, 1948 (63 of 1948). The premises used for manufacturing, processing, warehousing, packaging labeling and testing purposes shall be.

- Omitted by GOI Notification No. GSR 462(E) dt. 22.06.1982.
- Ins. by GOI Notification No. GSR 864(E) dt. 11.12.2001. applicable to manufacturers licensed to manufacture drugs, for the period up to 31.12.2003.

i. Compatible with other drug manufacturing operations that may be carried out in the same or adjacent area/section.

ii. Adequately provided with working space to allow orderly and logical placement of equipment, materials and movement of personnel so as to:

   a. Avoid the risk of mix-up between different categories of drugs or with raw materials, intermediates and in-process material.

   b. Avoid the possibilities of contamination and cross-contamination by providing suitable mechanism.

iii. Designed/constructed/maintained to prevent entry of insects, pests, birds, vermins, and rodents. Interior surface (walls, floors and ceilings) shall be smooth and free from cracks, and permit easy cleaning, painting and disinfection.

iv. Air-conditioned, where prescribed for the operations and dosage-forms under production. The production and dispensing areas shall be well lighted, effectively ventilated, with air control facilities and may have proper air handling units (wherever applicable) to maintain conditions including temperature, and wherever necessary, humidity, as defined for the relevant product. These conditions shall be appropriate to the category of drugs and nature of the operation. These shall also be suitable to the comforts of the personnel working with protective clothing, products handled, operations undertaken within them in relation to the external environment. These areas shall be regularly monitored for compliance with required specifications.

v. Provided with drainage system, as specified for the various categories of products, which shall be of adequate size and so designed as to prevent back flow and/or prevent insets and rodents entering the premises. Open channels shall be avoided in manufacturing areas, and where provided, these shall be shallow to facilitate cleaning and disinfection.

vi. The walls and floors of the areas where manufacture of drugs is carried out shall be free from cracks and open joints to avoid accumulation of dust. These shall be smooth, washable, covered and shall permit easy and effective cleaning and disinfection. The interior surfaces shall not shed particles. A periodical record of cleaning and painting of the premises shall be maintained.

1.3. ***Water system:*** There shall be validated system for treatment of water drawn from own or any other source to render it potable in accordance with standards specified by the Bureau of Indian Standards or Local Municipality, as the case may be, so as to produce purified water conforming to pharmacopoeial specification. Purified water so produced shall only be used for all operations except washing and cleaning operations where potable water may be used. Water shall be stored in tanks, which do not adversely affect quality of water and ensure freedom from microbiological growth. The tank shall be cleaned periodically and records maintained by the licensee in this behalf.

1.4. ***Disposal of waste***

i. The disposal of sewage and effluents (solid, liquid and gas) from the manufactory shall be in conformity with the requirements of Environment Pollution Control Board.
ii. All bio-medical waste shall be destroyed as per the provisions of the Bio-medical Waste (Management and Handling) Rules, 1996.
iii. Additional precautions shall be taken for the storage and disposal of rejected drugs. Records shall be maintained for all disposal of waste.
iv. Provisions shall be made for the proper and safe storage of waste materials awaiting disposal. Hazardous, toxic substances and flammable materials shall be stored in suitably designed and segregated, enclosed areas in conformity with Central and State Legislations.

2. Warehousing Area

2.1. Adequate areas shall be designed to allow sufficient and orderly warehousing of various categories of materials and products like starting and packaging materials, intermediates, bulk and finished products, products in quarantine, released, rejected, returned or recalled, machine and equipment spare parts and change items.

2.2. Warehousing areas shall be designed and adapted to ensure good storage conditions. They shall be clean, dry and maintained with acceptable temperature limits, where special storage conditions are required (e.g. temperature, humidity), these shall be provided, monitored and recorded. Storage areas shall have appropriate housekeeping and rodent, pests and vermin control procedures and records maintained. Proper racks, bins and platforms shall be provided for the storage of materials.

2.3. Receiving and dispatch bays shall protect materials and products from adverse weather conditions.

2.4. Where quarantine status is ensured by warehousing in separate earmarked areas in the same warehouse or store, these areas shall be clearly demarcated. Any system replacing the physical quarantine, shall give equivalent assurance of segregation. Access to these areas shall be restricted to authorized persons.

2.5. There shall be a separate sampling area in the warehousing area for active raw materials and excipients. If sampling is performed in any other area, it shall be conducted in such a way as to prevent contamination, cross-contamination and mix-up.

2.6. Segregation shall be provided for the storage of rejected, recalled or returned materials or products. Such areas, materials or products shall be suitably marked and secured. Access to these areas and materials shall be restricted.

2.7. Highly hazardous, poisonous and explosive materials such as narcotics, psychotropic drugs and substances presenting potential risks of abuse, fire or explosion shall be stored in safe and secure areas. Adequate fire protection measures shall be provided in conformity with the rules of the concerned civic authority.

2.8. Printed packaging materials shall be stored in safe, separate and secure areas.

2.9. Separate dispensing areas for (beta) lactam, sex hormones and cytotoxic substances or any such special categories of product shall be provided with proper supply of filtered air and suitable measures for dust control to avoid contamination. Such areas shall be under differential pressure.

2.10. Sampling and dispensing of sterile materials shall be conducted under aseptic conditions conforming to Grade A, which can also be performed in a dedicated area within the manufacturing facility.

2.11. Regular checks shall be made to ensure adequate steps are taken against spillage, breakage and leakage of containers.

2.12. Rodent treatments (pest control) should be done regularly and at least once in a year and record maintained.

3. Production Area

3.1. The production area shall be designed to allow the production preferably in uni-flow and with logical sequence of operations.

3.2. In order to avoid the risk of cross-contamination, separate dedicated and self-contained facilities shall be made available for the production of sensitive pharmaceutical products like penicillin or biological preparations with live microorganisms. Separate dedicated facilities shall be provided for the manufacture of contamination causing and potent products such as beta-lactam, sex hormones and cytotoxic substances.

3.3. Working and in-process space shall be adequate to permit orderly and logical positioning of equipment and materials and movement of personnel to avoid cross-contamination and to minimize risk of omission or wrong application of any manufacturing and control measures.

3.4. Pipe-work, electrical fittings, ventilation openings and similar services lines shall be designed, fixed and constructed to avoid creation of recesses. Services lines shall preferably be identified by colours and the nature of the supply and direction of the flow shall be marked/indicated.

4. Ancillary Areas

4.1. Rest and refreshment rooms shall be separate from other areas. These areas shall not lead directly to the manufacturing and storage areas.

4.2. Facilities for changing, storing clothes and for washing and toilet purposes shall be easily accessible and adequate for the number of users. Toilets, separate for males and females, shall not be directly connected with production or storage areas. There shall be written instructions for cleaning and disinfection of such areas.

4.3. Maintenance workshops shall be separate and away from production areas. Whenever spares, changed parts and tools are stored in the production area, these shall be kept in dedicated rooms or lockers. Tools and spare parts for use in sterile areas shall be disinfected before these are carried inside the production areas.

4.4. Areas housing animals shall be isolated from other areas. The other requirements regarding animal houses shall be those as prescribed in Rule 150-C(3) of the Drugs and Cosmetics Rules, 1945 which shall be adopted for production purposes.

5. Quality Control Area

5.1. Quality control laboratories shall be independent of the production areas. Separate areas shall be provided each for physicochemical, biological, microbiological or radioisotope analysis. Separate instrument room with adequate area shall be provided for sensitive and sophisticated instruments employed for analysis.

5.2. Quality control laboratories shall be designed appropriately for the operations to be carried out in them. Adequate space shall be provided to avoid mix-ups and cross-contamination. Sufficient and suitable storage space shall be provided for test samples, retained samples, reference standards, reagents and records.

5.3. The design of the laboratory shall take into account the suitability of construction materials and ventilation. Separate air handling units and other requirements shall be provided for biological, microbiological and radioisotopes testing areas. The laboratory shall be provided with regular supply of water of appropriate quality for cleaning and testing purpose.

5.4. Quality control laboratory shall be divided into separate sections, i.e. for chemical, microbiological and wherever required, biological testing. These shall have adequate area for basis installation and for ancillary purposes. The microbiology section shall have arrangements such as airlocks and laminar airflow workstation, wherever considered necessary.

6. Personnel

6.1. The manufacture shall be conducted under the direct supervision of competent technical staff with prescribed qualifications and practical experience in the relevant dosage and/or active pharmaceutical products.

6.2. The head of the quality control laboratory shall be independent of the manufacturing unit. The testing shall be conducted under the direct supervision of competent technical staff who shall be whole time employees of the licensee.

6.3. Personnel for quality assurance and quality control operations shall be suitably qualified and experienced.

6.4. Written duties of technical and quality control personnel shall be laid and following strictly.

6.5. Number of personnel employed shall be adequate and in direct proportion to the workload.

6.6. The licensee shall ensure in accordance with a written instruction that all personnel in production area or into quality control laboratories shall receive training appropriate to the duties and responsibility assigned to them. They shall be provided with regular in-service training.

7. Health, Clothing and Sanitation of Workers

7.1. The personnel handling beta-lactam antibiotics shall be tested for penicillin sensitivity before employment and those handling sex hormones, cytotoxic substances and other potent drugs shall be periodically examined for adverse effects. These personnel should be moved out of these sections (except in dedicated facilities), by rotation, as a health safeguard.

7.2. Prior to employment, all personnel, shall undergo medical examination including eye examination, and shall be free from tuberculosis, skin and other communicable or contagious diseases. Thereafter, they should be medically examined periodically, at least once a year. Records shall be maintained thereof. The licensee shall provide the services of a qualified physician for assessing the health status of personnel involved in different activities.

7.3. All persons prior to and during employment shall be trained in practices which ensure personnel hygiene. A high level of personal hygiene shall be observed by all those engaged in the manufacturing processes. Instructions to this effect shall be displayed in change rooms and other strategic locations.

7.4. No person showing, at any time, apparent illness or open lesions which may adversely affect the quality of products, shall be allowed to handle starting materials, packing materials, in-process materials, and drug products until his condition is no longer judged to be a risk.

7.5. All employees shall be instructed to report about their illness or abnormal health condition to their immediate supervisor so that appropriate action can be taken.

7.6. Direct contact shall be avoided between the unprotected hands of personnel and raw materials, intermediate or finished, unpacked products.

7.7. All personnel shall wear clean body coverings appropriate to their duties. Before entry into the manufacturing area, there shall be change rooms separate for each sex with adequate facilities for personal cleanliness such as wash basin with running water, clean towels, hand dryers, soaps, disinfectants, etc. The change room shall be provided with cabinets for the storage of personal belongings of the personnel.

7.8. Smoking, eating, drinking, chewing or keeping plants, food, drink and personal medicines shall not be permitted in production, laboratory, storage and other areas where they might adversely influence the product quality.

8. Manufacturing Operations and Controls

8.1. All manufacturing operations shall be carried out under the supervision of technical staff approved by the Licensing Authority. Each critical step in the process relating to the selection, weighing and measuring of raw material addition during various stages shall be performed by trained personnel under the direct personal supervision of approved technical staff. The contents of all vessels and containers used in manufacture and storage during the various manufacturing stages shall be conspicuously labeled with the name of the product, batch number, batch size and stage of manufacture. Each label should be initialled and dated by the authorised technical staff. Products not prepared under aseptic conditions are required to be free from pathogens like Salmonella, *Escherichia coli,* Pyocyanea, etc.

8.2. ***Precautions against mix-up and cross-contamination***

8.2.1. The licensee shall prevent mix-up and cross-contamination of drug material and drug product (from environmental dust) by proper air-handling system, pressure differential, segregation, status labeling and cleaning. Proper records and standard operating procedures thereof shall be maintained.

8.2.2. The licensee shall ensure processing of sensitive drugs like neta-lactam antibiotics, sex hormones and cytotoxic substances in segregated areas or isolated production areas within the building with independent air-handling unit and proper pressure differential. The effective segregation of these areas shall be demonstrated with adequate records of maintenance and services.

8.2.3. To prevent mix-ups during production stages, materials under process shall be conspicuously labeled to demonstrate their status. All equipment used for production shall be labeled with their current status.

8.2.4. Packaging lines shall be independent and adequately segregated. It shall be ensured that all leftovers of the previous packaging operations, including labels, cartons and caps are cleared before the closing hour.

8.2.5. Before packaging operations are begun, steps shall be taken to ensure that the work area, packaging lines, printing machines, and other equipment are clean and free from any products, materials and spillages. The line clearance shall be performed according to an approximate checklist and recorded.

8.2.6. The correct details of any printing (for example of batch numbers or expiry dates) done separately or in the course of the packaging shall be rechecked at regular intervals. All printing and overprinting shall be authorized in writing.

8.2.7. The manufacturing environment shall be maintained at the required levels of temperature, humidity and cleanliness.

8.2.8. Authorised persons shall ensure changeover into specific uniforms before undertaking any manufacturing operations including packaging.

8.2.9. There shall be segregated enclosed areas, secured for recalled or rejected material and for such materials which are to be reprocessed or recovered.

9. Sanitation in the Manufacturing Premises

9.1. The manufacturing premises shall be cleaned and maintained in an orderly manner, so that it is free from accumulated waste, dust, debris and other similar material. A validated cleaning procedure shall be maintained.

9.2. The manufacturing areas shall not be used for storage of materials, except for the material being processed. It shall not be used as a general throughfare.

9.3. A routine sanitation program shall be drawn up and observed, which shall be properly recorded and which shall indicate:

a. Specific areas to be cleaned and cleaning intervals.
b. Cleaning procedure to be followed, including equipment and materials to be used for cleaning.
c. Personnel assigned to and responsible for the cleaning operation.

9.4. The adequacy of the working and in-process storage space shall permit the orderly and logical positioning of equipment and materials so as to minimize the risk of mix-up between different pharmaceutical products or their components to avoid cross-contamination, and to minimise the risk of omission or wrong application of any of the manufacturing or control steps.

9.5. Production areas shall be well lit, particularly where visual online controls are carried out.

10. Raw Materials

10.1. The licensee shall keep an inventory of all raw materials to be used at any stage of manufacture of drugs and maintain records as per Schedule U.

10.2. All incoming materials shall be quarantined immediately after receipt or processing. All materials shall be stored under appropriate conditions and in an orderly fashion to permit batch segregation and stock rotation by a first in/first expiry first out principle. All incoming materials shall be checked to ensure that the consignment corresponds to the order placed.

10.3. All incoming materials shall be purchased from approved sources under valid purchase vouchers. Wherever possible, raw materials should be purchased directly from the producers.

10.4. Authorized staff appointed by the licensee in this behalf, which may include personnel from the quality control department, shall examine each consignment on receipt and shall check each container for integrity of package and seal. Damaged containers shall be identified, recorded and segregated.

10.5. If a single delivery of material is made up of different batches, each batch shall be considered as a separate batch for sampling, testing and release.

10.6. Raw materials in the storage area shall be appropriately labeled. Labels shall be clearly marked with the following information:

a. Designated name of the product and the internal code reference, where applicable, and analytical reference number.
b. Manufacturers name, address and batch number.
c. The status of the contents (e.g. quarantine, under test, released, approved, rejected).
d. The manufacturing date, expiry date and re-test date.

10.7. There shall be adequate separate areas for materials under test, approved and rejected with arrangements and equipment to allow dry, clean and orderly placement of stored materials and products, wherever necessary, under controlled temperature and humidity.

10.8. Containers from which samples have been drawn shall be identified.

10.9. Only raw materials which have been released by the quality control department and which are within their shelf-life shall be used. It shall be ensured that shelf life of formulation product shall not exceed with that of active raw materials used.

10.10. It shall be ensured that all the containers of raw materials are placed on the raised platforms/racks and not placed directly on the floor.

11. Equipment

11.1. Equipment shall be located, designed, constructed, adapted and maintained to suit the operations to be carried out. The layout and design of the equipment shall aim to minimise the risk of errors and permit effective cleaning and maintenance in order to avoid cross-contamination, build-up of dust or dirt, and in general any adverse effect on the quality of products. Each equipment shall be provided with a logbook, wherever necessary.

11.2. Balances and other measuring equipment of an appropriate range, accuracy and precision shall be available in the raw material stores, production and in-process control operations and these shall be calibrated and checked on a scheduled basis in accordance with standard operating procedures (SOPs) and records maintained.

11.3. The parts of the production equipment that come into contact with the product shall not be reactive, additive or adsorptive to an extent that would affect the quality of the product.

11.4. To avoid accidental contamination, wherever possible, non-toxic/edible grade lubricants shall be used and the equipment shall be maintained in a way that lubricants do not contaminate the products being produced.

11.5. Defective equipment shall be removed from production and quality control areas or appropriately labeled.

12. Documentation and Records

Documentation is an essential part of the quality assurance system, and as such, shall be related to all aspects GMPs. Its aim is to define the specifications for all materials, method of manufacture and control, to ensure that all personnel concerned with manufacture know the information necessary to decide whether or not to release a bath of drug for sale and to provide an audit trail that shall permit investigation of the history of any suspected defective batch.

12.1. Documents designed, prepared, reviewed and controlled, wherever applicable, shall comply with these rules.

12.2. Documents shall be approved, signed and dated by appropriate and authorized persons.

12.3. Documents shall specify the title, nature and purpose. They shall be laid out in an orderly fashion and be easy to check. Reproduced documents shall be clear and legible. Documents shall be regularly reviewed and kept up to date. Any alteration made in the entry of a document shall be signed and dated.

12.4. The records shall be made or completed at the time of each operation in such a way that all significant activities concerning the manufacture of pharmaceutical products are traceable. Records and associated SOPs shall be retained for at least one year after the expiry date of the finished product.

12.5. Data may be recorded by electronic data processing systems or other reliable means, but master formulae and detailed operating procedures relating to the system in use shall also be available in a hard copy to facilitate checking of the accuracy of the records. Wherever, documentation is handled by electronic data processing methods, authorized persons shall enter modify data in the computer. There shall be record of changed and deletions. Access shall be restricted by passwords. or other means and the result of entry of critical data shall be independently checked. Batch records electronically stored shall be protected by a suitable back-up. During the period of retention, all relevant data shall be readily available.

13. Labels and Other Printed Materials

Labels are absolutely necessary for identification of the drugs and their use. The printing shall be done in bright colours and in a legible manner. The label shall carry all the prescribed details about the product.

13.1. All containers and equipment shall bear appropriate labels. Different colour-coded tablets shall be used to indicate the status of a product (e.g. under test, approved, passed, rejected).

13.2. To avoid chance mix-up of printed packaging materials, product leaflets, relating to different products, shall be stored separately.

13.3. Prior to release, all labels for containers, cartons and boxes and all circulars, inserts and leaflets shall be examined by the quality control department of the licensee.

13.4. Prior to packaging and labeling of a given batch of a drug, it shall be ensured by the licensee that samples are drawn from the bulk and duly tested, approved and released by the quality control personnel.

13.5. Records of receipt of all labeling and packaging materials shall be maintained for each shipment received indicating receipt, control reference numbers and whether accepted or rejected. Unused coded and damaged labels and packaging materials shall be destroyed and recorded.

13.6. The label or accompanying document of reference standards and reference culture shall indicate concentration, lot number, potency, date on which containers was first opened and storage conditions, where appropriate.

14. Quality Assurance

This is a wide-ranging concept concerning all matters that individually or collectively influence the quality of a product. It is the totality of the arrangements made with the object of ensuring that products are of the quality required for their intended use.

14.1. The system of quality assurance appropriate to the manufacture of pharmaceutical products shall ensure that:

a. The pharmaceutical products are designed and developed in a way that takes account of the requirement of GMPs and other associated codes such as those of Good Laboratory Practices (GLPs) and Good Clinical Practices (GCPs).
b. Adequate arrangements are made for manufacture, supply and use of the correct starting and packaging materials.

c. Adequate controls on starting materials, intermediate products, and bulk products and other in-process controls, calibrations, and validations are carried out.
d. The finished product is correctly processed and checked in accordance with established procedures.
e. The pharmaceutical products are not released for sale or supplied before authorized persons have certified that each production batch as been produced and controlled in accordance with the requirements of the label claim and any other provisions relevant to production, control and release of pharmaceutical products.

15. Self-inspection and Quality Audit

It may be useful to constitute a self-inspection team supplemented with a quality audit procedure for assessment of all or part of a system with the specific purpose of improving it.

15.1. To evaluate the manufacturers compliance with GMP in all aspects of production and quality control, concept of self-inspection shall be followed. The manufacturer shall constitute a team of independent, experienced, qualified persons from within or outside the company, who can audit objectively the implementation of methodology and procedures evolved. The procedure for self-inspection shall be documented indicating self-inspection results; evaluation, conclusions and recommended corrective actions with effective follow-up program. The recommendations for corrective action shall be adopted.

15.2. The program shall be designed to detect shortcomings in the implementation of GMP and to recommend the necessary corrective actions. Self-inspection shall be performed routinely and on specific occasions, like when product recalls or repeated rejections occur or when an inspection by the licensing authorities is announced. The team responsible for self-inspection shall consist of personnel who can evaluate the implementation of GMP objectively. all recommendations for corrective action shall be implemented.

15.3. Written instructions for self-inspection shall be drawn up which shall include the following:

a. Personnel
b. Premises including personnel facilities

c. Maintenance of buildings and equipment
d. Storage of starting materials and finished products
e. Equipment
f. Production and in-process controls
g. Quality control
h. Documentation
i. Sanitation and hygiene
j. Validation and revalidation programmes
k. Calibration of instruments or measurement systems
l. Recall procedures
m. Complaints management
n. Labels control
o. Results of previous self-inspections and any corrective steps taken.

16. Quality Control System

Quality control shall be concerned with sampling, specifications, testing, documentation, release procedures which ensure that the necessary and relevant tests are actually carried and that the materials are not released for use, nor products released for sale or supply until their quality has been judged to be satisfactory. It is not confined to laboratory operations but shall be involved in all decisions concerning the quality of the product. It shall be ensured that all quality control arrangements are effectively and reliably carried out the department as a whole shall have other duties such as to establish evaluate, validate and implement all quality control procedures and methods.

16.1. Every manufacturing establishment shall establish its own quality control laboratory manner by qualified and experienced staff.

16.2. The area of the quality control laboratory may be divided into chemical, instrumentation, microbiological and biological testing.

16.3. Adequate area having the required storage conditions shall be provided for keeping reference samples. The quality control department shall evaluate, maintain and store reference samples.

16.4. Standard operating procedures shall be available for sampling, inspecting and testing of raw materials, intermediate bulk finished products and packing materials, and wherever necessary, for monitoring environmental conditions.

16.5. There shall be authorized and dated specifications for all materials, products, reagents and solvents including test of identity, content, purity and quality. These shall include specifications for water, solvents and reagents used in analysis.

16.6. No batch of the product shall be released for sale or supply until it has been certified by the authorized person(s) that it is in accordance with the requirements of the standards laid down.

16.7. Reference/retained samples from each batch of the products manufactured shall be maintained in quantity which is at least twice the quantity of the drug required to conduct all the tests, except sterility and pyrogen/bacterial endotoxin test performed on the active material and the product manufactured. The retained product shall be kept in its final pack or simulated pack for a period of three months after the date of expiry.

16.8. Assessment of records pertaining to finished products shall include all relevant factors, including the production conditions, the results of in-process testing, the manufacturing (including packaging) documentation, compliance with the specification for the finished product, and an examination of the finished pack. Assessment records should be signed by the incharge of production and countersigned by the authorised quality control personnel before a product is released for sale or distribution.

16.9. Quality control personnel shall have access to production areas for sampling and investigation, as appropriate.

16.10. The quality control department shall conduct stability studies of the products to ensure and assign their shelf-life at the prescribed conditions of storage. All records of such studies shall be maintained.

16.11. The incharge of quality assurance shall investigate all product complaints and records thereof shall be maintained.

16.12. All instruments shall be calibrated and testing procedures validated before these are adopted for routine testing. Periodical calibration of instrument and validation of procedures shall be carried out.

16.13. Each specification for raw materials, intermediates, final products, and packing materials shall be approved and maintained by the quality control department. Periodic revisions of the specifications shall be carried out wherever changes are necessary.

16.14. Pharmacopoeiae, reference standards, working standards, references, spectra, other reference materials and technical books, as required, shall be available in the quality control laboratory of the licensee.

17. Specification

17.1. *For raw materials and packaging materials*

a. They shall include the designated name and internal code reference.
b. Reference, if any, to a pharmacopoeial monograph.
c. Qualitative and quantitative requirements with acceptance limits.
d. Name and address of manufacturer or supplier and original manufacturer of the material.
e. Specimen of printed material.
f. Directions for sampling and testing or reference to procedures.
g. Storage conditions.
h. Maximum period of storage before re-testing.

17.2. *For product containers and closures*

17.2.1. All containers and closures intended for use shall comply with the pharmacopoeial requirements. Suitable validated test methods, sample sizes, specifications, cleaning procedure and sterilization procedure, wherever indicated, shall be strictly followed to ensure that these are not reactive, additive, absorptive, or leach to an extent that significantly affects the quality or purity of the drug. No second hand or used containers and closures shall be used.

17.2.2. Whenever bottles are being used, the written schedule of cleaning shall be laid down and followed. Where bottles are not dried after washing, they should be rinsed with de-ionised water or distilled water, as the case may be.

17.3. *For in-process and bulk products:* Specifications for in-process material, intermediate and bulk products shall be available. The specifications should be authenticated.

17.4. *For finished products:* Appropriate specifications for finished products shall include:

a. The designated name of the product and the code reference.
b. The formula or a reference to the formula and the pharmacopoeial reference.
c. Directions for sampling and testing or a reference to procedures.
d. A description of the dosage-form and package details.
e. The qualitative and quantitative requirements, with the acceptance limits for release.
f. The storage conditions and precautions, where applicable.
g. The shelf-life.

17.5. *For preparation of containers and closures:* The requirements mentioned in the Schedule do not include requirements of machinery, equipment and premises required for preparation of containers and closures for different dosage-forms and categories of drugs. The suitability and adequacy of the machinery, equipment and premises shall be examined taking into consideration the requirements of each licensee in this respect.

18. Master Formula Records

There shall be master formula records relating to all manufacturing procedures for each product and batch size to be manufactured. These shall be prepared and endorsed by the competent technical staff, i.e. head of production and quality control. The master formula shall include:

a. The name of the product together with product reference code relating to its specifications.

b. The patent or proprietary name of the product along with the generic name, a description of the dosage-form, strength, composition of the product and batch size.
c. Name, quantity, and reference number of all the starting materials to be used. Mention shall be made of any substance that may disappear in the courts of processing.
d. A statement of the expected final yield with the acceptable limits, and of relevant intermediate yields, where applicable.
e. A statement of the processing location and the principal equipment to be used.
f. The methods, or reference to the methods, to be used for preparing the critical equipment including cleaning, assembling, calibrating, and sterilizing.
g. Detailed stepwise processing instructions and the time taken for each step.
h. The instructions for in-process control with their limits.
i. The requirements for storage conditions of the products, including the container, labeling and special storage conditions where applicable.
j. Any special precautions to be observed.
k. Packing details and specimen labels.

19. Packing Records

There shall be authorised packaging instructions for each product, pack size and type. These shall include or have a reference to the following:

a. Name of the product.
b. Description of the dosage-form, strength and composition.
c. The pack size expressed in terms of the number of doses, weight or volume of the product in the final container.
d. Complete list of all the packaging materials required for a standard batch size, including quantities, sizes and types with the code of reference number relating to the specifications of each packaging material.
e. Reproduction of the relevant printed packaging materials and specimens indicating where batch number and expiry date of the product have been applied.

f. Special precautions to be observed, including a careful examination of the area and equipment in order to ascertain the line clearance before the operations begin.
g. Description of the packaging operation, including any significant subsidiary operations and equipment to be used.
h. Details of in-process controls with instructions for sampling and acceptance.
i. Upon completion of the packing and labeling operation, a reconciliation shall be made between number of labeling and packaging units issued, number of units labeled, packed and excess returned or destroyed. Any significant or unusual discrepancy in the numbers shall be carefully investigated before releasing the final batch.

20. Batch Packaging Records

20.1. A batch packaging record shall be kept for each batch or part batch processed. It shall be based on the relevant parts of the packaging instructions, and the method of preparation of such records shall be designed to avoid transcription errors.

20.2. Before any packaging operation begins, check shall be made and recorded that the equipment and the workstations are clear of the previous products, documents or materials not required for the planned packaging operations, and that the equipment is clean and suitable for use.

21. Batch Processing Records

21.1. There shall be batch processing record for each product. It shall be based on the relevant parts of the currently approved master formula. The method of preparation of such records included in the master formula shall be designed to avoid transcription errors.

21.2. Before any processing begins, check shall be performed and recorded to ensure that the equipment and workstation are clear of previous products, documents or materials not required for the planned process are removed and the equipment is clean and suitable for use.

21.3. During processing, the following information shall be recorded at the time each action is taken and the record shall be dated and signed by the person responsible for the processing operations:

a. The name of the product.
b. The number of the batch being manufactured.
c. Dates and time of commencement of significant intermediate stages and of completion of production.
d. Initials of the operator of different significant steps of production and where appropriate of the person who checked each of these operations.
e. The batch number and/or analytical control number as well as the quantities of each starting material actually weighed.
f. Any relevant processing operation or event and major equipment used.
g. A record of the in-process controls and the initials of the person(s) carrying them out, and the results obtained.
h. The amount of product obtained after different and critical stages of manufacture (yield).
i. Comments or explanations for significant deviations from the expected yield limits shall be given.
j. Notes on special problems including details, with signed authorization, for any deviation from the master formula.
k. Addition of any recovered or reprocessed material with reference to recovery or reprocessing stages.

22. Standard Operating Procedures (SOPs) and Records

22.1. ***Receipt of materials***

22.1.1. There shall be written standard operating procedures and records for the receipt of each delivery of raw, primary and printed packaging material.

22.1.2. The records of the receipts shall include:

a. The name of the material on the delivery note and the number of containers.
b. The date of receipt.
c. The manufacturers and/or suppliers name.
d. The manufacturers batch or reference number.

e. The total quantity, and number of containers, quantity in each container received.
f. The control reference number assigned after receipt.
g. Any other relevant comment or information.

22.1.3. There shall be written standard operating procedures for the internal labeling, quarantine and storage of starting materials, packaging materials and other materials, as appropriate.

22.1.4. There shall be standard operating procedures available for each instrument and equipment and these shall be placed in close proximity to the related instrument and equipment.

22.2. ***Sampling***

22.2.1. There shall be written standard operating procedures for sampling which include the person(s) authorized to take the samples.

22.2.2. The sampling instruction shall include:

a. The method of sampling and the sampling plan.
b. The equipment to be used.
c. Any precautions to be observed to avoid contamination of the material or any deterioration in its quality.
d. The quantity of samples to be taken.
e. Instructions for any required sub-division or poling of the samples.
f. The types of sample containers to be used.
g. Any specific precautions to be observed, especially in regard to sampling of sterile and hazardous materials.

22.3. ***Batch numbering***

22.3.1. There shall be standard operating procedures describing the details of the batch (lot) numbering set up with the objective of ensuring that each batch of intermediate, bulk or finished product is identified with a specific batch number.

22.3.2. Batch numbering standard operating procedures applied to a processing stage and to the respective packaging stage shall be same or traceable to demonstrate that they belong to one homogenous mix.

22.3.3. Batch number allocation shall be immediately recorded in a logbook or by electronic data processing system. The record shall include date of allocation, product identity and size of batch.

22.4. ***Testing***

22.4.1. There shall be written procedures for testing materials and products at different stages of manufacture, describing the methods and equipment to be used. The tests performed shall be recorded.

22.5. ***Records of analysis***

22.5.1. The records shall include the following data:

a. Name of the material or product and the dosage-form.
b. Batch number, and where appropriate the manufacturer and/or supplier.
c. Reference to the relevant specifications and testing procedures.
d. Test results including observations and calculations, and reference to any specifications (limits).
e. Dates of testing.
f. Initial of the persons who performed the testing.
g. Initial of the persons who verified the testing and the detailed calculations.
h. A statement of release or rejection.
i. Signature and date of the designated responsible person.

22.5.2. There shall be written standard operating procedures and the associated records of actions taken for:

a. Equipment assembly and validation
b. Analytical apparatus and calibration.
c. Maintenance, cleaning and sanitation.
d. Personnel matters including qualification, training, clothing, hygiene.
e. Environmental monitoring.
f. Pest control.
g. Complaints.
h. Recalls made.
i. Returns received.

23. Reference Samples

23.1. Each lot of every active ingredient, in a quality sufficient to carryout all the tests, except sterility and pyrogens/bacterial endotoxin test, shall be retained for a period of 3 months after the date of expiry of the last batch produced from that active ingredient.

23.2. Samples of finished formulations shall be stored in the same or simulated containers in which the drug has been actually marketed.

24. Reprocessing and Recoveries

24.1. Where reprocessing is necessary, written procedures shall be established and approved by the quality assurance department that shall specify the conditions and limitations of repeating chemical reactions. Such reprocessing shall be validated.

24.2. If the product batch has to be re-processed, the procedure shall be authorized and recorded. An investigation shall be carried out into the causes necessitating re-processing and appropriate corrective measures shall be taken for prevention of recurrence. Re-processed batch shall be subjected to stability evaluation.

24.3. Recovery of the product residue may be carried out, if permitted, in the master production and control records by incorporating it in subsequent batches of the product.

25. Distribution Records

25.1. Prior to distribution or dispatch of given batch of a drug, it shall be ensure that the batch has been duly tested, approved and released by the quality control personnel. Pre-dispatch inspection shall be performed on each consignment on a random basis to ensure that only the correct goods are dispatched. Detailed instructions for warehousing and stocking of large volume parenterals, if stocked, shall be in existence and shall be complied with after the batch is released for distribution. Periodic audits of warehousing practices followed at distribution centers shall be carried out and records thereof shall be maintained. Standard operating procedures shall be developed for warehousing of products.

25.2. Records for distribution shall be maintained in a manner such that finished batch of a drug can be traced to the retain level to facilitate prompt and complete recall of the batch, if and when necessary.

26. Validation and Process Validation

26.1. Validation studies shall be an essential part of GMPs and shall be conducted as per the pre-defined protocols. These shall include validation of processing, testing and cleaning procedures.

26.2. A written report summarizing recorded results and conclusions shall be prepared, documented and maintained.

26.3. Processes and procedures shall be established on the basis of validation study and undergo periodic revalidation to ensure that they remain capable of achieving the intended results. Critical processes shall be validated, prospectively for retrospectively.

26.4. When any new master formula or method of preparation is adopted, steps shall be taken to demonstrate its suitability for routine processing. The defined process, using the materials and equipment specified shall be demonstrated to yield a product consistently of the required quality.

26.5. Significant changes to the manufacturing process, including any changes in equipment or materials that may affect product quality and/or the reproducibility of the process, shall be validated.

27. Product Recalls

27.1. A prompt and effective product recall system of defective products shall be devised for timely information of all concerned stockists, wholesalers, suppliers, up to the retail level within the shortest period. The licensee may make use of both print and electronic media in this regard.

27.2. There shall be an established written procedure in the form of standard operating procedure for effective recall of products distributed by the licensee. Recall operations shall be capable of being initiated promptly so as to effectively reach at the level of each distribution channel.

27.3. The distribution records shall be readily made available to the persons designated for recalls.

27.4. The designated person shall record a final report issued, including reconciliation between the delivered and the recovered quantities of the products.

27.5. The effectiveness of the arrangements for recalls shall be evaluated from time to time.

27.6. The recalled products shall be stored separately in a secured segregated area pending final decision on them.

28. Complaints and Adverse Reactions

28.1. All complaints thereof concerning product quality shall be carefully reviewed and recorded according to written procedures. Each complaint shall be investigated/evaluated by the designated personnel of the company and records of investigation and remedial action taken thereof shall be maintained.

28.2. Reports of serious adverse drug reactions resulting from the use of a drug along with comments and documents shall be forthwith reported to the concerned licensing authority.

28.3. There shall be written procedure describing the action to be taken, recall to be made of the defective product.

29. Site Master File

The licensee shall prepare a succinct document in the form of site master file containing specific and factual GMPs about the production and/or control of pharmaceutical manufacturing preparations carried out at the licensed premises. It shall contain the following:

29.1. *General information*

a. Brief information of the firm.
b. Pharmaceutical manufacturing activities as permitted by the licensing authority.
c. Other manufacturing activities, if any, carried out on the premises.
d. Type of product licensed for manufacture with flow charts mentioning procedure and process flow.

e. Number of employees engaged in the production, quality control, storage and distribution.
f. Use of outside scientific, analytical or other technical assistance in relation to manufacture and analysis.
g. Short description of the quality management system of the firm.
h. Products detail registered with foreign countries.

29.2. ***Personnel***

a. Organisational chart showing the arrangement for quality assurance including production and quality control.
b. Qualification, experience and responsibilities of key personnel.
c. Outline for arrangements for basic and in-service training and how the records are maintained.
d. Health requirements for personnel engaged in production.
e. Personal hygiene requirements, including clothing.

29.3. ***Premises***

a. Simple plan or description of manufacturing areas drawn to scale.
b. Nature of construction and fixtures/fittings.
c. Brief description of ventilation systems. More details should be given for critical areas with potential risk of airborne contamination (schematic drawing of systems). Classification of the rooms used for the manufacture of sterile products should be mentioned.
d. Special areas for the handling of the highly toxic, hazardous and sensitizing materials.
e. Brief description of water system (schematic drawings of systems), including sanitation.
f. Description of planned preventive maintenance programs for premises and of the recording system.

29.4. ***Equipment***

a. Brief description of major equipment used in production and quality control laboratories (a list of equipment required).
b. Description of planned preventive maintenance programs for equipment and of the recording system.

c. Qualification and calibration including the recording systems and arrangements for computerized systems validation.

29.5. *Sanitation*

a. Availability of written specifications and procedures for cleaning manufacturing areas and equipment.

29.6. *Documentation*

a. Arrangements for the preparation, revision and distribution of.
b. Necessary documentation for the manufacture.
c. Any other documentation related to product quality that is not mentioned elsewhere (e.g. microbiological controls about air and water).

29.7. *Production*

a. Brief description of production operations using, wherever possible, flow sheets and charts specifying important parameters.
b. Arrangements for the handling of starting materials, packaging materials, bulk and finished products, including sampling, quarantine, release and storage.
c. Arrangements for the handling of rejected materials and products.
d. Brief description of general policy for process validation.

29.8. *Quality control*

a. Description of the quality control system and of the activities of the quality control department. Procedures for the release of the finished products.

29.9. *Loan licence manufacture and licensee*

a. Description of the way in which compliance of GMPs by the loan licensee shall be assessed.

29.10. *Distribution, complaints and product recall*

a. Arrangements and recording system for distribution.
b. Arrangements for handling of complaints and product recalls.

29.11. *Self-inspection*

a. Short description of the self-inspection system indicating whether an outside, independent and experienced external export was involved in evaluating the manufacturers compliance with GMPs in all aspects of production.

29.12. *Export of drugs*

a. Products exported to different countries.
b. Complaints and product recall, if any.

PART I-A

Specific Requirements for Manufacture of Sterile Products, Parenteral Preparations (Small Volume Injectables and Large Volume Parenterals) and Sterile Ophthalmic Preparations

Note: *The general requirements as given in Part I of this Schedule relating to requirements of GMPs for premises and materials for pharmaceutical products shall be complied with, mutatis mutandis, for the manufacture of sterile products, parenteral preparations (small volume injectables and large volume parenterals) and sterile ophthalmic preparations. In addition to these requirements, the following specific requirements shall also be followed.*

1. General

Sterile products, being very critical and sensitive in nature, a very high degree of precautions, prevention and preparations and needed. Dampness, dirt and darkness are to be avoided to ensure aseptic conditions in all areas. There shall be strict compliance in the prescribed standards especially in the matter of supply of water, air, active materials and in the maintenance of hygienic environment.

2. Building and Civil Works

2.1. The building shall be built on proper foundation with standardized materials to avoid cracks in critical areas like aseptic solution preparation, filling and sealing rooms.

2.2. Location of services like water, steam, gases, etc. shall be such that their servicing or repair shall not pose any threat to the integrity of the facility. Water lines shall not pose any threat of leakage to aseptic area.

2.3. The manufacturing areas shall be clearly separated into support areas (e.g. washing and component preparation areas, storage areas, etc.), preparation areas (e.g. bulk manufacturing area, non-aseptic blending areas, etc.), change areas and aseptic areas. Operations like removal of outer cardboard wrappings of primary packaging materials shall be done in the de-cartoning areas which are segregated from the washing areas. Wooden pallets, fiberboard drugs, cardboard and other particle shedding materials shall not be taken inside the preparation areas.

2.4. ***In aseptic areas***

a. Walls, floors and ceiling should be impervious, non-shedding, non-flaking and non-cracking. Flooring should be unbroken and provided with a cove both at the junction between the wall and the floor as well as the wall and ceiling.

b. Walls shall be flat, and ledges and recesses shall be avoided. Wherever other surfaces join the wall (e.g. sterilizers, electric sockets, gas points, etc.), these shall flush the walls. Walls shall be provided with a cove at the joint between the ceiling and floor.

c. Ceiling shall be solid and joints shall be sealed. Light-fittings and air-grills shall flush with the walls and not hanging from the ceiling, so as to prevent contamination.

d. There shall be no sinks and drains in Grade A and Grade B areas.

e. Doors shall be made of non-shedding material. These may be made preferably of aluminium or steel material. Wooden doors shall not be used. Doors shall open towards the higher pressure area so that they close automatically due to air pressure.

f. Windows shall be made of similar material as the doors, preferably with double panel and shall be flush with the walls. If fire escapes are to be provided, these shall be suitably fastened to the walls without any gaps.

g. The furniture used shall be smooth, washable and made of stainless steel or any other appropriate material other than wood.

2.5. The manufacturing and support areas shall have the same quality of civil structure described above for aseptic areas, except the environmental standards which may vary in the critical areas.

2.6. Change rooms with entrance in the form of air-locks shall be provided before entry into the sterile product manufacturing areas and then to the aseptic area. Separate exit space from the aseptic areas is advisable. Change rooms to the aseptic areas shall be clearly demarcated into black gray, and white rooms with different levels of activity and air cleanliness. The black change room shall be provided with a handwashing sink. The sink and its drain in the unclassified (first) change rooms may be kept clean all the time. The specially designed drain shall be periodically monitored to avoid presence of pathogenic microorganisms. Change room doors shall not be opened simultaneously. An appropriate interlocking system and a visual and/or audible warning system may be installed to prevent the opening of more than one door at a time.

2.7. For communication between aseptic areas and non-aseptic areas, intercom telephones or speak-phones shall be used. These shall be minimum in number.

2.8. Material transfer between aseptic areas and outside shall be through suitable airlocks or pass-boxes. Doors of such airlocks and pass-boxes shall have suitable interlocking arrangements.

2.9. Personal welfare areas like rest rooms, tea room, canteen and toilets shall be outside and separated from the sterile product manufacturing area.

2.10. Animal houses shall be away from the sterile product manufacturing area and shall not share a common entrance or air handling system with the manufacturing area.

3. Air Handling System (Central Air-conditioning)

3.1. Air handling units for sterile product manufacturing areas shall be different from those for other areas. Critical areas, such as the aseptic filling area, sterilized components unloading area and change room conforming to Grades B, C and D respectively shall have separate air handling units. The filter configuration in the air handling system shall be suitably designed to achieve the Grade of air as given in Table 8.1. Typical operational activities for clean areas are highlighted in Tables 8.2 and 8.3.

3.2. For products which are filled aseptically, the filling room shall meet Grade B conditions at rest unmanned. This condition shall also be obtained within a period of about 30 minutes of the personnel leaving the room after completion of operations.

3.3. The filling operations shall take place under Grade A conditions which shall be demonstrated under working of simulated conditions which shall be achieved by providing laminar airflow workstations with suitable HEPA filters or isolator technology.

3.4. For products, which are terminally sterilized, the filling room shall meet Grade C conditions at rest. This condition shall be obtainable within a period of about 30 minutes of the personnel leaving the room after completion of operations.

3.5. Manufacturing and component preparation areas shall meet Grade C conditions.

3.6. After completion of preparation, washed components and vessels shall be protected with Grade C background and if necessary, under laminar airflow workstation.

3.7. The minimum air changes for Grade B and Grade C areas shall not be less than 20 air changes per hour in a room with good airflow pattern and appropriate HEPA filters. For Grade A laminar airflow workstations, the airflow rate shall be 0.3 meter per second ± 20% (for vertical flows) and 0.45 meter per second ± 20% (for horizontal flows).

3.8. Differential pressure between areas of different environmental standards shall be at least 15 Pascal (0.06 inches or 1.5 mm water gauge). Suitable manometers or gauges shall be installed to measure and verify pressure differential.

3.9. The final change room shall have the same class or air as specified for the aseptic area. The pressure differentials in the change rooms shall be in the descending order from white to black.

3.10. Unless there are product specific requirements, temperature and humidity in the aseptic areas shall not exceed 27°C and relative humidity 55%, respectively.

Table 8.1: Airborne particulate classification for manufacture of sterile products

	Maximum number of permitted particles per cubic metre equal to or above			
	At rest		*In operation*	
Grade	*0.5 μm*	*5.0 μm*	*0.5 μm*	*5.0 μm*
A	3,520	29	3,500	29
B	35,200	293	3,52,000	2,930
C	3,52,000	2,930	35,20,000	29,300
D	3,52,0000	29,300	Not defined	Not defined

Notes

(a) *In order to reach the B, C and D air grades, the number of air changes shall be* related to the size of the room and the equipment and personnel present in the room. The air system shall be provided with the appropriate filters such as HEPA for Grades A, B and C. The maximum permitted number of particles in the "at rest" condition shall approximately be as under: Grade A corresponds with Class 100 or M 3.5 or ISO Class 5. Grade B with Class 1000 or M 4.5 or ISO Class 6. Grade C with Class 10,000 or M 5.5 or ISO Class 7. Grade D with Class 100,000 or M 6.5 or ISO Class 8.

(b) *The requirement and limit for the area shall depend on the nature of the operation* carried out.

(c) *Type of operations to be carried out in the various grades are given in Tables 8.2 and 8.3.*

Table 8.2: Types of operations to be carried out in the various grades for aseptic preparations

Grade	*Types of operations for aseptic preparations*
A	Aseptic preparation and filling
B	Background room conditions for activities requiring Grade A
C	Preparation of solution to be filtered
D	Handling of components after washing

Table 8.3: Types of operations to be carried out in the various grades for terminally sterilized products

Grade	*Types of operations for terminally sterilized products*
A	Filling of products, which are usually at risk
C	Placement of filling and sealing machines, preparation of solutions when usually at risk. Filling of product when unusually at risk
D	Moulding, blowing (pre-forming) operations of plastic containers, preparations of solutions and components for subsequent filling

4. Environmental Monitoring

4.1. All environmental parameters are listed under Para 3.1 to 3.10 shall be verified and established at the time of installation and thereafter monitored at periodic intervals. The recommended frequencies of periodic monitoring shall be as follows:

a. Particulate monitoring in air — 6 monthly
b. HEPA filter integrity testing (smoke testing) — Yearly
c. Air change rates — 6 monthly
d. Air pressure differentials — Daily
e. Temperature and humidity — Daily
f. Microbiological monitoring by settle plates and/or swabs in aseptic areas daily, and at decreased frequency in other areas

Note: *The above frequencies of monitoring shall be changed as per the requirements and load in individual cases.*

4.2. There shall be a written environmental monitoring program and microbiological results shall be recorded. Recommended limits for microbiological monitoring of clean areas in operation are given in Table 8.4.

Table 8.4. Recommended limits for microbiological monitoring of clean areas in operation

Grade	*Air sample*	*Settle plates (dia. 90 mm) cfu/4 hours*	*Contact plates (dia. 55 mm) cfu/plate*	*Glove points 5 fingers cfu/glove*
A	< 1	< 1	< 1	< 1
B	10	5	5	5
C	100	50	25	–
D	500	100	50	–

Notes

a. These are average values.
b. Individual settle plates may be exposed for not less than two hours in Grade B, C and D areas and for not less than thirty minutes in Grade A area.

4.3. Appropriate action shall be taken immediately if the result of particulate and microbiological monitoring indicates that the counts exceed the limits. The standard operating procedures shall contain corrective action. After major engineering modification to the HVAC system of any area, all monitoring shall be re-performed before production commences.

5. Garments

5.1. This section covers garments required for use by personnel working only in aseptic area. Outdoor clothing shall not be brought into the sterile areas.

5.2. The garments shall be made of non-shedding and tight weave material. Cotton garments shall not be used. The garments shall shed virtually no fibres or particulate matter.

5.3. The clothing and its quality shall be adopted to the process and the workplace and worn in such a way as to protect the product from contamination. Garments shall be single piece with fastenings at cuffs, neck and at legs to ensure close fit. Trouser legs shall be tucked inside the cover boots. Suitable design of garments shall either include a hood (head-cover) or a separate hood which can be tucked inside the overall. Pockets, pleats and belts shall be avoided in garments. Zips (if any) shall be of plastic material. Garments with damaged zips shall not be used.

5.4. Only clean, sterilized and protective garments shall be used at each work session where aseptic filtration and filling operations are undertaken and at each work shift for products intended to be sterilized, post-filling. The mask and gloves shall be changed at every work session in both instances.

5.5. Gloves shall be made of latex or other suitable plastic materials and shall be powder-free. These shall be long enough to cover wrists completely and allow the overall cuff to be tucked in.

5.6. The footwear shall be of suitable plastic or rubber material and shall be daily cleaned with a bactericide.

5.7. Safety goggles or numbered glasses with side extension shall be used inside aseptic areas. These shall be sanitized by a suitable method.

5.8. Garment changing procedures shall be documented and operators trained in this respect. A full size mirror shall be provided in the final change room for the operator to verify that he is appropriately attired in the garments. Periodic inspection of the garments shall be done by responsible staff.

6. Sanitation

6.1. There shall be written procedures for the sanitation of sterile processing facilities. Employees carrying out sanitation of aseptic areas shall be trained specifically for this purpose.

6.2. Different sanitizing agent shall be used in rotation and the concentrations of the same shall be as per the recommendations of the manufacturer. Records of rotational use of sanitizing agents shall be maintained.

6.3. Distilled water freshly collected directly from the distilled water plant or water maintained above 70°C from the re-circulation loop shall be used for dilution of disinfectants. Alternatively, distilled water sterilized by autoclaving or membrane filtration shall be used. The dilution shall be carried out in the white change room.

6.4. Where alcohol or isopropyl alcohol is used for dilution of disinfectants for use as hand sprays, the preparation of the same shall be done in the bulk preparation area and diluted solution membrane filtered into suitable sterile containers held in aseptic area.

6.5. Diluted disinfectants shall bear the label use before, based on microbiological establishment of the germicidal properties. The solutions shall be adequately labeled and documents maintained.

6.6. Formaldehyde or any other equally effective fumigant is recommended for the fumigation of aseptic areas or after major civil modifications. There shall be standard operating procedures for this purpose. Its use for routine purpose shall be discouraged and an equally effective surface cleaning regime shall be followed.

6.7. Cleaning of sterile processing facilities shall be undertaken with air suction devices or with non-linting sponges or clothes.

6.8. Air particulate quality shall be evaluated on a regular basis and record maintained.

7. Equipment

7.1. The special equipment required for manufacturing sterile products includes component washing machines, steam sterilizers, dry heat sterilizers, membrane filter assemblies, manufacturing vessels, blenders, liquid filling machines, powder filling machines, sealing and labeling machines, vacuum testing chambers, inspection machines, lyophilisers, pressure vessels, etc. suitable and fully integrated washing sterilizing filling lines may be provided, depending upon the type and volume of activity.

7.2. Unit sterilizers shall be double-ended with suitable interlocking arrangements between the doors. The effectiveness of the sterilization process shall be established initially by biological inactivation studies using microbial spore indicators and then at least once a year by carrying out thermal mapping of the chamber. Various sterilization parameters shall be established based on these studies and documented. For membrane filters used for filtration, appropriate filter integrity tests that ensure sterilization shall be carried out before and after filtration.

7.3. Filling machines shall be challenged initially and then at periodic intervals by simulation trials including sterile media fill. Standard operating procedures and acceptance criteria for media fills shall be established, justified and documented.

Special simulation trial procedures shall be developed, validated and documented for special products like ophthalmic ointments.

7.4. The construction material used for the parts which are in direct contact with products and the manufacturing vessels may be stainless steel 316 or borosilicate glass (if glass containers) and the tubing shall be capable of being washed and autoclaved.

7.5. On procurement, installation qualification of each of the equipment shall be done by engineers with the support of production and quality assurance personnel. Equipment for critical processes like aseptic filling and sterilizers shall be suitably validated according to a written program before putting them to use.

7.6. Standard operating procedures shall be available for each equipment for its calibration and operation and cleaning. Gauges and other measuring devices attached to equipment shall be calibrated at suitable intervals against a written program. Calibration status of equipment gauges shall be adequately documented and displayed.

8. Water and Steam Systems

8.1. Potable water meeting microbiological specification of not more than 500 cfu/ml and indicating absence of individual pathogenic microorganisms, *Escherichia coli*, Salmonella, *Staphylococcus aureus and Pseudomonas aeruginosa* per 100 ml sample shall be used for the preparation of purified water.

8.2. Purified water prepared by demineralization shall meet the microbiological specification of not more than 100 cfu per ml and indicate absence of pathogenic micro-organisms in 100 ml. Purified water shall also meet IP specification for chemical quality. Purified water shall be used for handwashing in change rooms. Containers, closures and machine parts may be washed with potable water followed by suitably filtered purified water. Purified water shall be stored in stainless steel tanks or plastic tanks.

8.3. Water for injection (hereinafter as WFI) shall be prepared from potable water or purified water meeting the above specifications by distillation. Water for injection shall meet microbiological specification of not more than 10 cfu per

100 ml. WFI shall also met IP specification for water for injection and shall have an endotoxin level of not more than 0.25 EU/ml. Bulk solutions of liquid parenterals shall be made in WFI. Final rinse of product containers and machine parts shall be done with WFI. Disinfectant solutions for use in aseptic areas shall be prepared in WFI.

8.4. Water for injection for the manufacture of liquid injectables shall be freshly collected from the distillation plant or from a storage or circulation loop where the water has been kept at above 70°C. At the point of collection, water may be cooled using suitable heat exchanger.

8.5. Water for non-injectable sterile products like eye drops shall meet IP specifications for purified water. In addition, microbiological specification of not more than 10 cfu per 100 ml and absence of *Pseudomonas aeruginosa* and *Enterobacter coli* in 100 ml shall also be met.

8.6. Water for injection shall be stored in steam jacketed stainless steel tanks of suitable size and the tanks shall have hydrophobic bacterial retention with 0.2 μ vent filters. The filters shall be suitably sterilized at periodic intervals. The distribution lines for purified water and distilled water shall be of stainless steel 316 construction and shall not shed particles.

8.7. There shall be a written procedure and program for the sanitation of different water systems including storage tanks, distribution lines, pumps and other related equipment. Records of sanitation shall be maintained.

8.8. There shall be written microbiological monitoring program for different types of water. The results shall justify the frequency of sampling and testing. Investigation shall be carried out and corrective action taken in case of deviation from prescribed limits.

8.9. Steam coming in contact with the product, primary containers and other product contact surfaces shall be sterile and pyrogen free. The steam condensate shall meet microbiological specification of not more than 10 cfu per 100 ml. the condensate shall also meet IP specification for water for injection and shall have an endotoxin levels of not more than 0.25 EU/ml. There shall be a suitable schedule for the monitoring of steam quality.

9. Manufacturing Process

9.1. Manufacture of sterile products shall be carried out only in areas under defined conditions.

9.2. Bulk raw materials shall be monitored for bioburden periodically. Bioburden of bulk solution prior to membrane filtration shall be monitored periodically and a limit of not more than 100 cfu per ml is recommended.

9.3. The time between the start of the preparation of the solution and its sterilization or filtration through a micro-organism retaining filter shall be minimized. There shall be a set maximum permissible time for each product that takes into account its composition and method of storage mentioned in the master formula record.

9.4. Gases coming in contact with the sterile product shall be filtered through two 0.22 μ hydrophobic filters connected in-series. These filters shall be tested for integrity. Gas cylinders shall not be taken inside aseptic areas.

9.5. Washed containers shall be sterilized immediately before use. Sterilized containers, if not used within an established time, shall be rinsed with distilled or filtered purified water and re-sterilized.

9.6. Each lot of finished product shall be filled in one continuous operation. In each case, where one batch is filled in using more than one operation, each lot shall be tested separately for sterility and held separately till sterility test results are known.

9.7. Special care shall be exercised while filling products in powder form so as not to contaminate the environment during transfer of powder to filling machine-hopper.

10. Form-Fill-Seal Technology or Blow and Fill-Seal Technology

10.1. Form-fill-seal units are specially built automated machines in which through one continuous operation, containers are formed from thermoplastic granules, filled and then sealed. Blow, fill-seal units are machines in which containers are moulded/blown (pre-formed) in separate clean rooms, by non-continuous operations.

Note

i. *These shall be installed in at least Grade C environment.*
ii. *These shall comply with the limits as recommended in Table at Item 4.2.*

10.2. Form-fill-seal/blow, fill-seal machines used for the manufacture of products for terminal sterilization shall be installed in at least Grade C environment and the filling zone within the machine shall fulfill Grade A requirements.

10.3. ***Terminally sterilized products***

10.3.1. Preparation of primary packaging material such as glass bottles, ampoules and rubber stoppers shall be done in at least Grade D environment. Where there is unusual risk to the product from microbial contamination, the above operation shall be done in Grade C environment. All the process used for component preparation shall be validated.

10.3.2. Filling of products requiring terminal sterilization shall be done under Grade A environment with a Grade C background.

10.4. Preparation of solutions, which is to be sterilized by filtration, shall be done in Grade C environment, and if not to be filtered, the preparation of materials and products shall be in a Grade A environment with Grade B in background.

10.5. ***Filtration (membrane)***

i. Solutions for large volume parenterals shall be filtered through a non-fibre releasing, sterilizing grade cartridge/membrane filter of nominal pore size of 0.22 μ for aseptic filling whereas 0.45 μ porosity shall be used for terminally sterilized products.
ii. A second filtration using another 0.22 μ sterilizing grade cartridge/membrane filter shall be performed immediately prior to filling. Process specifications shall indicate the maximum time during which a filtration system may be used with a view to precluding microbial build-up to levels that may affect the microbiological quality of the large volume parenterals.

iii. The integrity of the sterilized filter shall be verified and confirmed immediately after use by an appropriate method such as bubble point, diffusive flow or pressure hold test.

10.6. ***Sterilization (autoclaving)***

10.6.1. Before any sterilization process is adopted, its suitability for the product and its efficacy in achieving the desired sterilizing conditions in all parts of each type of load pattern to be processed, shall be demonstrated by physical measurements and by biological indicators, where appropriate.

10.6.2. All the sterilization process shall be appropriately validated. The validity of the process shall be verified at regular intervals, but at least annually. Whenever significant modifications have been made to the equipment and product, records shall be maintained thereof.

10.6.3. The sterilizer shall be double-ended to prevent mix-ups.

10.6.4. Periodic bioburden monitoring of products before terminal sterilization shall be carried out and controlled to limits specified for the product in the master formula.

10.6.5. The use of biological indicators shall be considered as an additional method of monitoring the sterilization. These shall be stored and used according to the manufacturer's instructions. Their quality shall be checked by positive controls. If biological indicators used, strict precautions shall be taken to avoid transferring microbial contamination from them.

10.6.6. There shall be clear means of differentiating sterilized/ unsterilized products. Each basket, tray or other carrier of products or components shall be clearly labeled with the name of the material, its batch number, and sterilization status. Indicators shall be used, where appropriate, to indicate whether a batch (or sub-batch) has passed through the sterilization process.

10.6.7. Sterilization records shall be available for each sterilization run and may also include thermographs and sterilization monitoring strips. They shall be maintained as part of the batch release procedure.

10.7. ***Sterilization (by dry heat)***

10.7.1. Each heat sterilization cycle shall be recorded on a time/temperature chart of a suitable size by appropriate equipment of the required accuracy and precision. The position of temperature probes used for controlling and/or recording shall be determined during the validation, and where applicable, shall also be checked against a second independent temperature probe located in the same position. The chart shall form a part of the batch record. Container mapping may also be carried out in the case of large volume parenterals.

10.7.2. Chemical or biological indicators may also be used, but shall take the place of physical validation.

10.7.3. Sufficient time shall be allowed for the load to reach the required temperature before measurement of sterilization time commences. This time shall be separately determined for each type of load to be processed.

10.7.4. After the high temperature phase of a heat sterilization cycle, precautions shall be taken against contamination of sterilized load during cooling. Any cooling fluid or gas in contact with the product shall be sterilized unless it can be shown that any leaking container would not be approved for use. Air inlet and outlets shall be provided with bacterial retaining filters.

10.7.5. The process used for sterilization by dry heat shall include aircirculation within the chamber and the maintenance of a positive pressure to prevent the entry of non-sterile air. Air inlets and outlets should be provided with micro-organism retaining filters. Where this process of sterilization by dry heat is also intended to remove pyrogens, challenge tests using endotoxins would be required as part of the validation process.

10.8. ***Sterilization (by moist heat)***

10.8.1. Both the temperature and pressure shall be used to monitor the process. Control instrumentation shall normally be independent of monitoring instrumentation and recording charts. Where automated control and monitoring systems are used for these applications, these shall be validated to ensure that critical process requirements are met. System and cycle faults shall be registered by the system and observed by the operator. The reading of the independent temperature indicator shall be routinely checked against the chart-recorder during the sterilization period. For sterilizers fitted with a drain at the bottom of the chamber, it may also be necessary to record the temperature at this position throughout the sterilization period. There shall be frequent leak tests done on the chamber during the vacuum phase of the cycle.

10.8.2. The items to be sterilized, other than products in sealed containers, shall be wrapped in a material which allows removal of air and penetration of steam but which prevents re-contamination after sterilization. All parts of the load shall be in contact with the sterilizing agent at the required temperature of the required time.

10.8.3. No large volume parenteral shall be subjected to steam sterilization cycle until it has been filled and sealed.

10.8.4. Care shall be taken to ensure that the steam used for sterilization is of a suitable quality and does not contain additives at a level which could cause contamination of the product or equipment.

10.9. ***Completion/finalisation of sterile products***

10.9.1. All unit operations and processes in the manufacture of a batch shall have a minimum time specified and the shortest validated time shall be used from the start of a batch to its ultimate release for distribution.

10.9.2. Containers shall be closed by appropriately validated methods. Containers closed by fusion, e.g. glass or plastic ampoules shall be subjected to 100% integrity testing. Samples of other containers shall be checked for integrity according to appropriate procedures.

10.9.3. Containers sealed under vacuum shall be tested for required vacuum conditions.

10.9.4. Filled containers parenteral products shall be inspected individually for extraneous contamination or other defects. When inspection is done visually, it shall be done under suitably controlled conditions of illumination and background. Operators doing the inspection shall pass regular eye-sight checks with spectacles, if worn, and be allowed frequent rest from inspection. Where other methods of inspection are used, the process shall be validated and the performance of the equipment checked at suitable intervals. Results shall be recorded.

11. Product Containers and Closures

11.1. All containers and closures intended for use shall comply with the pharmacopoeial and other specified requirements. Suitable samples sizes, specifications, test methods, cleaning procedures and sterilization procedures, shall be used to assure that containers, closures and other component parts of drug packages are suitable and are not reactive, additive, adsorptive or leachable or presents the risk of toxicity to an extent that significantly affects the quality or purity of the drug. No second hand or used containers and closures shall be used.

11.2. Plastic granules shall also comply with the pharmacopoeial requirements including physiochemical and biological tests.

11.3. All containers and closures shall be rinsed prior to sterilization with water for injection according to written procedure.

11.4. The design of closures, containers and stoppers shall be such as to make cleaning, easy and also to make airtight seal when fitted to the bottles.

11.5. It shall be ensured that containers and closures chosen for a particular product are such that when coming into contact they are not absorbed into the product and they do not affect the product adversely. The closures and stoppers should be of such quality substances as not to affect the quality of the product and avoid the risk of toxicity.

11.6. Whenever glass bottles are used, the written schedule of cleaning shall be laid down and followed. Where bottles are not dried after washing, these shall be finally rinsed with distilled water or pyrogen free water, as the case may be, according to written procedure.

11.7. Individual containers of parenteral preparations, ophthalmic preparations shall be examined against black/white background fitted with diffused light after filling so as to ensure freedom from foreign matters.

11.8. *Glass bottles*

11.8.1. Shape and design of the glass bottle shall be rational and standardized. Glass bottles made of USP Type I and USP Type II glass shall only be used. Glass bottles shall not be reused. Before use, USP Type II bottles shall be validated for the absence of particulate matter generated over a period of the shelf-life of the product and shall be regularly monitored after the production, following statistical sampling methods. USP Type III glass containers may be used for non-parenteral sterile products such as otic solutions.

11.9. *Plastic containers*

11.9.1. Pre-formed plastic containers intended to be used for packing of large volume parenteral shall be moulded in-house by one continuous operation through an automatic machine.

11.9.2. Blowing, filling and sealing (plugging) operation shall be conducted in room(s) conforming to requirements as mentioned in Table 8.3 of item 3.10. Entry to the area where such operations are undertaken, shall be through a series of airlocks. Blowers shall have an air supply which is filtered through 0.22 μ filters. Removal of runners and plugging operations shall be conducted under a laminar airflow workstation.

11.10. *Rubber stoppers*

11.10.1. The tuber stoppers used for large volume parenterals shall comply with specifications prescribed in the current edition of the Indian Pharmacopoeia.

12. Documentation

12.1. The manufacturing records relating to manufacture of sterile products shall indicate the following details:

1. Serial number of the batch manufacturing record.
2. Name of the product.
3. Reference to master formula record.
4. Batch/lot number

5. Batch/lot size.
6. Date of commencement of manufacture and date of completion of manufacture.
7. Date of manufacture and assigned date of expiry.
8. Date of each step in manufacturing.
9. Name of all ingredients with the grade given by the quality control department.
10. Quality of all ingredients.
11. Control reference numbers for all ingredients.
12. Time and duration of blending, mixing, etc. whenever applicable.
13. pH of solution whenever applicable.
14. Filter integrity testing records
15. Temperature and humidity records whenever applicable
16. Records of plate counts whenever applicable.
17. Results of pyrogen and/or bacterial endotoxin and toxicity.
18. Results of weight or volume of drug filled in containers.
19. Bulk sterility in case of aseptically filled products.
20. Leak test records.
21. Inspection records.
22. Sterilization records including autoclave leakage test records, load details, date, duration, temperature, pressure, etc.
23. Container washing records.
24. Total number of containers filled.
25. Total numbers of containers rejected at each stage
26. Theoretical yield, permissible yield, actual yield and variation thereof.
27. Clarification for variation in yield beyond permissible yield.
28. Reference numbers of relevant analytical reports.
29. Details of reprocessing, if any.
30. Name of all operators carrying out different activities.
31. Environmental monitoring records.
32. Specimens of printed packaging materials.

33. Records of destruction of rejected containers printed packaging and testing.
34. Signature of competent technical staff responsible for manufacture and testing.

Note

1. *Products shall be released only after complete filling and testing.*
2. *Result of the tests relating to sterility, pyrogens, and bacterial endotoxins shall be maintained in the analytical records.*
3. *Validation details and simulation trail records shall be maintained separately.*
4. *Records of environmental monitoring like temperature, humidity, microbiological data, etc. shall be maintained. Records of periodic servicing of HEPA filters, sterilizers and other periodic maintenance of facilities and equipment carried out also be maintained.*
5. *Separate facilities shall be provided for filling-cum-sealing of small volume parenterals in glass containers and/or plastic containers.*
6. *It is advisable to provide separate facilities for manufacture of large volume parenterals in glass containers and/or plastic containers.*
7. *For manufacture of large volume parenterals in plastic containers, it is advisable to install automatic (with all operations) form-fill-seal machines having one continuous operation.*

PART I-B

Specific Requirements for Manufacture of Oral Solid Dosage-Forms (Tablets and Capsules)

Note: The general requirements as given in Part I of this Schedule relating to requirements of GMPs for premises and materials for pharmaceutical products shall be complied with, mutates mutandis, for the manufacture of oral solid dosage-forms (tablets and capsules). In addition to these requirements, the following specific requirement shall also be followed.

1. General

1.1. The processing of dry materials and products creates problems of dust control and cross-contamination. Special attention is therefore, needed in the design, maintenance and use of premises and equipment in order to overcome these problems. Wherever required, enclosed dust control manufacturing systems shall be employed.

1.2. Suitable environmental conditions for the products handled shall be maintained by installation of air-conditioning wherever necessary. Effective air extraction systems, with discharge points situated to avoid contamination of other products and professes shall be provided. Filters shall be installed to retain dust and protect the factory and local environment.

1.3. Special care shall be taken to protect against subsequent contamination of the product by particles of metal or wood. The use of metal detector is recommended. Wooden equipment should be avoided. Screens, sieves, punches and dies shall be examined for wear and tear or for breakage before and after each use.

1.4. All ingredients for a dry product shall be sifted before use unless the quality of the input material can be assured. Such sifting shall normally be carried out at dedicated areas.

1.5. Where the facilities are designed to provide special environmental conditions of pressure differentials between rooms, these conditions shall be regularly monitored and any specification results brought to the immediate attention of the production and quality assurance department which shall be immediately attended to.

1.6. Care shall be taken to guard against any material lodging and remaining undetected in any processing or packaging equipment. Particular care shall be taken to ensure that any vacuum, compressed air or air-extraction nozzles are kept clean and that there is no evidence lubricants leaking into the product from any part of the equipment.

2. Sifting, Mixing and Granulation

2.1. Unless operated as a closed system, mixing, sifting and blending equipment shall be fitted with dust extractors.

2.2. Residues from sieving operations shall be examined periodically for evidence of the presence of unwanted materials.

2.3. Critical operating parameters like time and temperature for each mixing, blending and drying operation shall be specified in a master formula, monitored during processing, and recorded in the batch records.

2.4. Filter bags fitted to fluid-bed drier shall not be used for different products, without being washed in-between use. With certain highly potent or sensitizing products, bags specific to one product only shall be used. Air entering the drier shall be filtered. Steps shall be taken to prevent contamination of the site and local environment by dust in the air leaving the drier due to close positioning of the air-inlets and exhaust.

2.5. Granulation and coating solutions shall be made, stored and used in a manner which minimizes the risk of contamination or microbial growth.

3. Compressions (Tablets)

3.1. Each tablets compressing machine shall be provided with effective dust control facilities to avoid cross-contamination. Unless the same product is being made on each machine, or unless the compression machine itself provides its own enclosed air-controlled environment, the machine shall be installed in separate cubicles.

3.2. Suitable physical,, procedural and labeling arrangements shall be made to prevent mix-up of materials, granules and tables on compression machinery.

3.3. Accurate and calibrated weighing equipment shall be readily available and used for in-process monitoring of tablet weight variation. Procedures used shall be capable of detecting out-of-limits tablets.

3.4. At the commencement of each compression run and in case of multiple compression points in a compression machine, sufficient individual tablets shall be examined at fixed intervals to ensure that a tablet from each compression station or from each compression point has been inspected for suitable pharmacopoeial parameters like appearance, weight variation, disintegration, hardness, friability and thickness. The results shall be recorded as part of the batch documentation.

3.5. Tablets shall be de-dusted, preferably by automatic device and shall be monitored for the presence of foreign materials besides any other defects.

3.6. Tablets shall be collected into clean, labeled containers.

3.7. Rejected or discarded tablets shall be isolated in identified containers and their quality recorded in the batch manufacturing record.

3.8. In-process control shall be employed to ensure that the products remain within specification. During compression, samples of tablets shall be taken at regular intervals of not greater than 30 minutes to ensure that they are being produced in compliance with specified in-process specification. The tablets shall also be periodically checked for additional parameters such as appearance, weight variation, disintegration, hardness, friability and thickness and contamination by lubricating oil.

4. Coating (Tablets)

4.1. Air supplied to coating pans for drying purposes shall be filtered air and of suitable quality. The area shall be provided with suitable exhaust system and environmental control (temperature, humidity) measures.

4.2. Coating solutions and suspensions shall be made afresh and used in a manner, which shall minimize the risk of microbial growth. Their preparation and use shall be documented and recorded.

5. Filling of Hard Gelatin Capsule

Empty capsules shells shall be regarded as drug component. treated accordingly. They shall be stored under conditions which shall ensure their safety from the effects of excessive heat and moisture.

6. Printing (Tablets and Capsules)

6.1. Special care shall be taken to avoid product mix-up during any printing of tablets and capsules. Where different products, or different batches of the same product, are printed simultaneously, the operations shall adequately be segregated. Edible grade colours and suitable printing ink shall be used for such printing.

6.2. After printing, tablets and capsules shall be approved by quality control before release for packaging or sale.

7. Packaging (Strip and Blister)

7.1. Care shall be taken when using automatic tablet and capsule counting, strip and blister packaging equipment to ensure that all rogue tablets, capsules or foils from packaging operation are removed before a new packaging operation is commenced. There shall be an independent recorded check of the equipment before a new batch of tablets or capsules is handled.

7.2. Uncoated tablets shall be packed on equipment designed to minimize the risk of cross-contamination. Such packaging shall be carried out in an isolated area when potent tablets or beta-lactam containing tablets are being packed.

7.3. The strips coming out of the machine shall be inspected for defects such as misprint, cuts on the foil, missing tablets and improper sealing.

7.4. Integrity of individual packaging strips and blisters shall be subjected to vacuum test periodically to ensure leak proofness of each pocket strip and blister and records maintained.

PART I-C

Specific Requirements for Manufacture of Oral Liquids (Syrups, Elixirs, Emulsions and Suspensions)

Note: *The general requirements as given in Part I of this Schedule relating to requirements of GMPs for premises and materials for pharmaceutical products shall be complied with, mutates mutandis, for the manufacture of (syrups, elixirs, emulsions and suspensions). In addition to these requirements, the following specific requirements shall also be followed.*

1. Building and Equipment

1.1. The premises and equipment shall be designed, constructed and maintained to suit the manufacturing of oral liquids. The layout and design of the manufacturing area shall strive to minimize the risk of cross-contamination and mix-ups.

1.2. Manufacturing area shall have entry through double door airlock facility. It shall be fly proof by use of fly catcher and/or air curtain.

1.3. Drainage shall be of adequate size and have adequate traps, without open channels and design shall be such as to prevent back flow. Drains shall be shallow to facilitate cleaning and disinfecting.

1.4. The production area shall be cleaned and sanitized at the end of every production process.

1.5. Tanks, containers, pipe work and pumps shall be designed and installed so that they can be easily cleaned and sanitized. Equipment design shall be such as to prevent accumulation of residual microbial growth or cross-contamination.

1.6. Stainless steel or any other appropriate material shall be used for parts of equipment coming in direct contact with the products. The use of glass apparatus shall be minimum.

1.7. Arrangements for cleaning of containers, closures and droppers shall be made with the help of suitable machines/ devices equipped with the high pressure air, water and steam jets.

1.8. The furniture used shall be smooth, washable and made up of stainless steel.

2. Purified Water

2.1. The chemical and microbiological quality of purified water used shall be specified and monitored routinely. The microbiological evaluation shall include testing for absence of pathogens and shall not exceed 100 cfu/ml (as per Appendix 12.5 of IP 1996).

2.2. There shall be a written procedure for operation and maintenance of the purified water system. Care shall be taken to avoid the risk of microbial proliferation with appropriate methods like re-circulation, use of UV treatment, treatment with heat and sanitizing agent. After any chemical sanitisation of the water systems, a flushing shall be done to ensure that the sanitizing agent has been effectively removed.

3. Manufacturing

3.1. Manufacturing personnel shall wear non-fiber shedding clothing to prevent contamination of the product.

3.2. Materials likely to shed fiber-like gunny bags, or wooden pallets shall not be carried into the area where products or cleaned-containers are exposed.

3.3. Care shall be taken to maintain the homogenecity of emulsion by use of appropriate emulsifier and suspensions by use of appropriate stirrer during filling. Mixing and filling processes shall be specified and monitored. Special care shall be taken at the beginning of the filling process, after stoppage due to any interruption and at the end of the process to ensure that the product is uniformly homogenous during the filling process.

3.4. The primary packaging area shall have an air supply which is filtered through 5 micron filters. The temperature of the area shall not exceed 30°C.

3.5. When the bulk product is not immediately packed, the maximum period of storage and storage conditions shall be specified in the master formula. The maximum period of storage time of a product in the bulk stage shall be validated.

PART I-D

Specific Requirements for Manufacture of Topical Products, i.e. External Preparations (Creams, Ointments, Pastes, Emulsions, Lotions, Solutions, Dusting Powders and Identical Products)

Note: *The general requirements as given in Part I of this Schedule relating to requirements of GMPs for premises and materials for pharmaceutical products shall be complied with, mutates mutandis, for the manufacture of topical products, i.e. external preparations (creams, ointments, pastes, emulsions, lotions, solutions, dusting powders and identical products used for external applications). In addition to these requirements, following specific requirements shall also be followed.*

1. The entrance to the area where topical products are manufactured should be through a suitable airlock. Outside the airlock, insectocutors shall be installed.
2. The air to this manufacturing area shall be filtered through at least 20 μ air filters and shall be air-conditioned. The area shall be ventilated.
3. The area shall be fitted with an exhaust system of suitable capacity to effectively remove vapours, fumes, smoke, floating dust particles.
4. The equipment used shall be designed and maintained to prevent the product from being accidentally contaminated with any foreign matter or lubricant.
5. No rags or dusters shall be used in the process of cleaning or drying the process equipment or accessories used.
6. Water used in compounding shall be purified water IP.
7. Powders, wherever used, shall be suitably sieved before use.
8. Heating vehicles and a base-like petroleum jelly shall be done in separate mixing area in suitable stainless steel vessels, using steam, gas, electricity, solar energy, etc.
9. A separate packing section may be provided for primary packaging of the products.

PART I-E

Specific Requirements for Manufacture of Metered-Dose-Inhalers (MDI)

Note: *The general requirements as given in Part I of this Schedule relating to requirements of GMPs for premises and materials for pharmaceutical products shall be complied with, mutates mutandis, for the manufacture of metered-dose-inhalers (MDI). In addition to these requirements, the following specific requirements shall also be followed.*

1. General

Manufacture of metered-dose-inhalers shall be done under conditions which shall ensure minimum microbial and particulate contamination. Assurance of the quality of components and the bulk product is very important. Where medicaments are in suspended state, uniformity of suspension shall be established.

2. Building and Civil Works

2.1. The building shall be located on a solid foundation to reduce risk of cracking walls and floor due to the movement of equipment and machinery.

2.2. All building surfaces shall be impervious, smooth and non-shedding. Flooring shall be continuous and provided with a cove between the floor and the wall as well as the wall to the ceiling. Ceiling shall be solid, continuous and covered to walls. Light fittings and air-grills shall be flush with the ceiling. All service lines requiring maintenance shall be erected in such a manner that these accessible from outside the production area.

2.3. The manufacturing area shall be segregated into change rooms for personnel, container preparation area, bulk preparation and filling area, quarantine area and spray testing and packing areas.

2.4. Secondary change rooms shall be provided for operators to change from factory clothing to special departmental clothing before entering the manufacturing and filling areas.

2.5. Separate area shall be provided for de-cartoning of components before they are air washed.

2.6. The propellants used for manufacture shall be delivered to the manufacturing area distribution system by filtering them through 2 μ filters. The bulk containers of propellants shall be stored, suitably identified, away from the manufacturing facilities.

3. Environmental Conditions

3.1. Where products or clean components are exposed, the area shall be supplied with filtered air of Grade C.

3.2. The requirements of temperature and humidity in the manufacturing area shall be decided depending on the type of product and propellants handled in the facility. Other support area shall have comfort levels of temperature and humidity.

3.3. There shall be a difference in room pressure between the manufacturing and support areas and the differential pressure shall be not less than 15 Pascals (0.06 inches or 1.5 mm water gauge).

3.4. There shall be a written schedule for the monitoring of environmental conditions. Temperature and humidity shall be monitored daily.

4. Garments

4.1. Personnel in the manufacturing and filling section shall wear suitable single-piece-garment made out of non-shedding, tight weave material. Personnel in support areas shall wear clean factory uniforms.

4.2. Gloves made up of suitable material having no interaction with the propellants shall be used by the operators in the manufacturing and filling areas. Preferably, disposable gloves shall be used.

4.3. Suitable department-specific personnel protective equipment like footwear and safety glasses shall be used wherever hazard exists.

5. Sanitation

5.1. There shall be written procedures for the sanitation of the MDI manufacturing facility. Special care should be taken to handle residues and rinses of propellants.

5.2. Use of water for cleaning shall be restricted and controlled. Routinely used disinfectants are suitable for sanitizing the different areas. Records of sanitation shall be maintained.

6. Equipment

6.1. Manufacturing equipment shall be of closed system. The vessels and supply lines shall be of stainless steel.

6.2. Suitable check weights, spray testing machines and labeling machines shall be provided in the department.

6.3. All the equipment shall be suitably calibrated and their performance validated on receipt and thereafter periodically.

7. Manufacture

7.1. There shall be approved master formula records for the manufacture of metered-dose-inhalers. All propellants, liquids and gases shall be filtered through 2 µ filters to remove particles.

7.2. The primary packing material shall be appropriately cleaned by compressed air suitably filtered through 0.2 μ filter. The humidity of compressed air shall be controlled as applicable.

7.3. The valves shall be carefully handled and after de-cartoning, there shall be kept in clean, closed containers in the filling room.

7.4. For suspensions, the bulk shall be kept stirred continuously.

7.5. In-process controls shall include periodical checking of weight of bulk formulation filled in the containers. In a two-shot-filling process (liquid filling followed by gaseous filling), it shall be ensured that 100% check on weight is carried out.

7.6. Filled containers shall be quarantined for a suitable period established by the manufacturer to detect leaking containers prior to testing, labeling and packing.

8. Documentation

8.1. In addition to the routine good manufacturing practices documentation, manufacturing records shall show the following additional information:

1. Temperature and humidity in the manufacturing area.
2. Periodic filled weights of the formulation.
3. Records of rejections during online check weighing.
4. Records of rejection during spray testing.

PART I-F

Specific Requirements of Premises, Plant and Materials for Manufacture of Active Pharmaceutial Ingredients (Bulk Drugs)

Note: *The general requirements as given in Part I of this Schedule relating to Requirements of GMPs for premises and materials for pharmaceutical products shall be complied with, mutates mutandis, for the manufacture of active pharmaceutical ingredients (bulk drugs). In addition to these requirements, the following specific requirements shall also be followed.*

1. Building and Civil Works

1.1. Apart from the building requirements contained Part I, general note, the active pharmaceutical ingredients facilities for manufacture of hazardous reactions, beta-lactam antibiotics. Steroids and steroidal hormones/cytotoxic substances shall be provided in confined areas to prevent contamination of the other drugs manufactured.

1.2. The final stage of preparation of a drug, like isolation/ filtration/drying/milling/sieving and packing operations shall be provided with air filtration systems including pre-filters and finally with a 5-micron filter. Air handling systems with adequate number of air changes per hour or any other suitable system to control the airborne contamination shall be provided. Humidity/temperature shall also be controlled for all the operations wherever required.

1.3. Air filtration systems including pre-filters and particulate matter retention air filters shall be used, where appropriate, for air supplies to production areas. If air is recirculated to production areas, measures shall be taken to control re-circulation of floating dust particles from production. In areas where air contamination occurs during production, there shall be adequate exhaust system to control contaminants.

1.4. Ancillary area shall be provided for boilerhouse. Utility areas like heat exchangers, chilling workshop, store and supply of gases shall also be provided.

1.5. For specified preparation like manufacture of sterile products and for certain antibiotics, sex hormones, cytotoxic and oncology products, separate enclosed areas shall be designed. The requirements for the sterile active pharmaceutical ingredient shall be in-line with the facilities required for formulation to be filled aseptically.

2. Sterile Products

Sterile active pharmaceutical ingredient filled aseptically shall be treated as formulation from the stage wherever the process demands like crystallization, lyophilisation, filtration, etc. All conditions applicable to formulations that are required to be filled aseptically shall apply *mutates mutandis* for the manufacture of sterile active pharmaceutical ingredients involving stages like filtration crystallization and lyophilisation.

3. Utilities/Services

Equipment like chilling plant, boiler, heat exchangers, vacuum and gas storage vessels shall be serviced, cleaned, sanitized and maintained at appropriate intervals to prevent malfunctions or contamination that may interfere with safety, identity, strength, quality or purity of the drug product.

4. Equipment Design, Size and Location

4.1. Equipment used in the manufacture, processing, packing or holding of an active pharmaceutical ingredient shall be of appropriate design, adequate size and suitably located to facilitate operations for its intended use and for its cleaning and maintenance.

4.2. If the equipment is used for different intermediates and active pharmaceutical ingredients, proper cleaning before switching from one product to another becomes particularly important. If cleaning of a specific type of equipment is difficult, the equipment may need to be dedicated to a particular intermediate or active pharmaceutical ingredient.

4.3. The choice of cleaning methods, detergents and levels of cleaning shall be defined and justified. Selection of cleaning agents (e.g. solvents) should depend on:

a. The suitability of the cleaning agent to remove residues of raw materials, intermediates, precursors, degradation products and isomers, as appropriate.
b. Whether the cleaning agent leaves a residue itself.
c. Compatibility with equipment construction materials like centrifuge/filtration, dryer/fluid bed dryer, rotocone proton dryer, vacuum dryer, frit mill, multi-mill/jet mills/sewetters cut sizing.
d. Test for absence of intermediate or active pharmaceutical ingredient in the final rinse.

4.4. Written procedures shall be established and followed for cleaning and maintenance of equipment, including utensils used in the manufacture, processing, packing or holding of active pharmaceutical ingredients. These procedures shall include but should not be limited to the following:

a. Assignment of responsibility for cleaning and maintaining equipment.
b. Maintenance and cleaning program schedules, including where appropriate, sanitizing schedules.
c. A complete description of the methods and materials used to clean and maintain equipment, including instructions for de-assembling and reassembling each article of equipment to ensure proper cleaning and maintenance.
d. Removal or obliteration of previous batch identification.
e. Protection of clean equipment from contamination prior to use.
f. Inspection of equipment for cleanliness immediately before use.
g. Establishing the maximum time that may elapse between completion of processing and equipment cleaning as well as between cleaning and equipment reuse.

4.5. Equipment shall be cleaned between successive batches to prevent contamination and carry-over of degraded material or contaminants unless otherwise established by validation.

4.6. As processing approaches the final purified active pharmaceutical ingredient, it is important to ensure that incidental carry-over between batches does not have adverse impact on the established impurity profile. However, this does not generally hold good for any biological, active pharmaceutical ingredient where many of the processing steps are accomplished aseptically and where it is necessary to clean and sterilize equipment between batches.

5. In-process Controls

5.1. In-process control for chemical reactions may include the following:

a. Reaction time or reaction completion.
b. Reaction mass appearance, clarity, completeness or pH solutions.
c. Reaction temperature.
d. Concentration of a reactant.
e. Assay or purity of the product.
f. Process completion check by TLC/any other means.

5.2. In-process control for physical operations may include the following:

a. Appearance and colour.
b. Uniformity of the blend.
c. Temperature of a process.
d. Concentration of a solution.
e. Processing rate or time.
f. Particle size analysis.
g. Bulk/tap density.
h. pH determination.
i. Moisture content.

6. Product Containers and Closures

6.1. All containers and closures shall comply with the pharmacopoeial or any other requirement, suitable sampling methods, sample sizes, specifications, test methods, cleaning procedures and sterilization procedures, when indicated, shall be used to assure that containers, closures and other component parts of drug packages are suitable and are not reactive, additive, adsorptive or leachable to an extent that significantly affects the quality or purity of the drug.

6.2. The drug product container shall be tested or re-examined as appropriate and approved or rejected and shall be identified and controlled under a quarantine system designed to prevent their use in manufacturing or processing operations for which these are unsuitable.

6.3. Container closure system shall provide adequate protection against foreseeable external factors in storage/transportation and use that may cause deterioration or contamination of the active pharmaceutical ingredient.

6.4. Bulk containers and closures shall be cleaned and, where indicated by the nature of the active pharmaceutical ingredient, sterilized to ensure that they are suitable for their intended use.

6.5. The container shall be conspicuously marked with the name of the product and the following additional information concerning:

a. Quality and standards, if specified.

b. Manufacturing licence number/drug master file number (whichever applicable), batch number.
c. Date of manufacture and date of expiry.
d. Method for container disposal (label shall give the methodology, if required).
e. Storage conditions, if specified and name and address of the manufacturer, if available.

6.6. Areas for different operation of active pharmaceutical ingredients (bulk drugs) section shall have appropriate area which may be suitably partitioned for different operations.

PART II

Requirements of Plant and Equipment

1. External Preparations

The following pieces of equipment are recommended for the manufacture of external preparations, i.e. ointments, emulsion, lotions, solutions, pastes, creams, dusting powders and such identical products used for external applications whichever is applicable, namely:

1. Mixing and storage tanks (stainless steel).
2. Jacketted kettle (steam, gas or electrically heated).
3. Mixer (electrically operated).
4. Planetary mixer.
5. A colloid mill or a suitable emulsifier.
6. A triple roller mill or an ointment mill.
7. Liquid filling equipment (electrically operated).
8. Jar or tube filling equipment (electrically operated).

Area

1. A minmum area of thirty square meters for basic installation of ten square meters for ancillary area is recommended.
2. Areas for formulations meant for external use and internal use shall be separately provided to avoid mix-up.

2. Oral Liquid Preparations

The following pieces of equipment are recommended for the manufacture of oral/internal use preparations, i.e. syrups, elixirs, emulsions and suspensions, whichever is applicable, namely:

1. Mixing and storage tanks (stainless steel).
2. Jacketted kettle/stainless steel tank (steam, gas or electrically heated).
3. Portable stirrer (electrically operated).
4. A colloid mill or suitable emulsifier (electrically operated).
5. Suitable filtration equipment (electrically operated).
6. Semi-automatic/automatic bottle filling machine.
7. Pilfer-proof cap sealing machine.
8. Water distillation unit or deioniser.
9. Clarity testing inspection units.

Area

A minimum area of thirty square meters for basic installation and ten square meters for ancillary area is recommended.

3. Tablets

The tableting section shall be free from dust and floating particles and may be air-conditioned. For this purpose, each tablet machine shall be isolated into cubicles and connected to a vacuum dust collector or an exhaust system. For effective operations, the tablet production department shall be divided into four distinct and separate sections as follows:

a. Mixing, granulation and drying section.
b. Tablet compression section.
c. Packaging section (strip/blister machine wherever required).
d. Coating section (wherever required).

3.1. The following electrically operated pieces of equipment are recommended for the manufacture of compressed tablets and hypodermic tablets, in each of the above sections, namely:

a. Granulation-cum-drying section
    1. Disintegrator and sifter.
    2. Powder mixer.
    3. Mass mixer/planetary mixer/rapid mixer granulator.
    4. Granulator.
    5. Thermostatically controlled hot air oven with trays (preferably mounted on a trolley)/fluid bed dryer.
    6. Weighing machines.

b. Compression section:
   1. Tablet compression machine, single/multi-punch/ rotatory.
   2. Punch and dies storage cabinets.
   3. Tablet de-duster
   4. Tablet inspection unit/belt.
   5. Dissolution test apparatus
   6. In-process testing equipment like single pan electronic balance, hardness tester, friability and disintegration test apparatus.
   7 Air-conditioning and dehumidification arrangement (wherever necessary).

c. Packaging section:
   1. Strip/blister packaging machine.
   2. Leak test apparatus (vacuum system)
   3. Tablet counters (wherever applicable)
   4. Air-conditioning and dehumidification arrangement (wherever applicable).

Area

A minimum area of sixty square meters for basic installation and twenty square meters for ancillary area is recommended for un-coated tablets.

d. Coating section:
   1. Jacketted kettle (steam, gas or electrically heated for preparing coating suspension).
   2. Coating pan (stainless steel).
   3. Polishing pan (where applicable).
   4. Exhaust system (including vacuum dust collector).
   5. Air-conditioning and dehumidification arrangement.
   6. Weighing balance.

3.2. The coating section shall be made dust free with suitable exhaust system to remove excess powder and fumes resulting from solvent evaporation. It shall be air-conditioned and dehumidified wherever considered necessary.

Area

A minimum additional area of thirty square meters for coating section for basic installation and ten square meters for ancillary area is recommended. Separate area and equipment for mixing, granulation, drying, tablet compression, coating and packing shall be provided for penicillin group of drugs on the lines indicated above. In case of operations involving dust and floating particles, care shall be exercised to avoid cross-contamination.

3.3. The manufacture of hypodermic tablets shall be conducted under aseptic conditions in a separate air-conditioned room, the walls of which shall be smooth and washable. The granulation, tableting and packing shall be done in this room.

3.4. The manufacture of effervescent and soluble/dispersible tablets shall be carried out in air-conditioned and dehumidified areas.

4. Powders

The following pieces of equipment are recommended for the manufacture of powders, namely:

1. Disintegrator.
2. Mixer (electrically operated).
3. Sifter.
4. Stainless steel vessels and scoops of suitable sizes.
5. Filling equipment (electrically operated).
6. Weighing balance.

In the case of operation involving floating particles of fine powder, suitable exhaust system shall be provided. Workers should be provided with suitable masks during operation.

Area

A minimum area of thirty square meters is recommended to allow for the basic installations. Where the actual blending is to be done on the premises, an additional room shall be provided for the purpose.

5. Capsules

For the manufacture of capsules, separate enclosed area suitably air-conditioned and dehumidified with an airlock arrangement shall be provided. The following pieces of equipment are recommended for filling hard gelatin capsules, namely:

1. Mixing and blending equipment (electrically or power driven).
2. Capsules filling units (preferably semi-automatic or automatic filling machines).
3. Capsules counters (wherever applicable).
4. Weighing balance.
5. Disintegration test apparatus.
6. Capsule polishing equipment.

Separate equipment, and filling and packaging area shall be provided in penicillin and non-penicillin sections. In case of operations involving floating particles of fine powder, a suitable exhaust system shall be provided. Manufacture and filling shall be carried out in air-conditioned area. The room shall be dehumidified.

Area

A minimum area of twenty-five square meters for basic installation and ten square meters for ancillary area each for penicillin and non-penicillin sections is recommended.

6. Surgical Dressing

The following pieces of equipment are recommended for the manufacture of surgical dressings other than absorbent cotton wool, namely:

1. Rolling machine.
2. Trimming machine.
3. Cutting equipment.
4. Folding and pressing machine for gauze.
5. Mixing tanks for processing medicated dressing.
6. Hot air dry oven.
7. Steam sterilizer or dry heat sterilizer or other suitable equipment.
8. Work tables/benches for different operations.

Area

A minimum area of thirty square meters is recommended to allow for the basic installations. In case medicated dressings are to be manufactured, another room with a minimum area of thirty square meters shall be provided.

7. Ophthalmic Preparations

For the manufacture of ophthalmic preparations, separate enclosed areas with airlock arrangement shall be provided. The following pieces of equipment are recommended for the manufacture under aseptic conditions of eye-ointment, eye-lotions and other preparations for external use, namely:

1. Thermostatically controlled hot air ovens (preferably double ended).
2. Jacketted kettle/stainless steel tanks (steam, gas or electrically heated).
3. Mixing and storage tanks of stainless steel/planetary mixer.
4. Colloid mill or ointment mill.
5. Tube filling and crimping equipment (semi-automatic or automatic filling machines).
6. Tube cleaning equipment (air jet type).
7. Tube washing and drying equipment, if required.
8. Automatic vial washing machine.
9. Vial drying oven.
10. Rubber bung washing machine.
11. Sintered glass funnel, Seitz filter and filter candle (preferably cartridge and membrane filters).
12. Liquid filling equipment (semi-automatic or automatic filling machines).
13. Autoclave (preferably ventilator autoclave).
14. Air-conditioning and dehumidification arrangement (preferably centrally air-conditioned and dehumidification system).
15. Laminar airflow units.

Area

1. A minimum area of twenty-five square meters for basic installation and ten square meters for ancillary area is recommended. Manufacture and filling shall be carried out in air-conditioned areas under aseptic conditions. The rooms shall be further dehumidified as considered necessary if preparations containing antibiotics are manufactured.
2. Areas for formulations meant for external use and internal use shall be separately provided to avoid mix up.

8. Pessaries and Suppositories

i. The following pieces of equipment are recommended for manufacture of pessaries and suppositories, namely:
   1. Mixing and pouring equipment
   2. Moulding equipment.
   3. Weighing devices.

Area

A minimum area of twenty square meters is recommended to allow for the basic installation.

iii. In the case of pessaries manufactured by granulation and compression, the requirements as indicated under item 3 of tablet, shall be provided.

9. Inhalers and Vitrallae

The following pieces of equipment are recommended for manufacture of inhalers and vitrallae, namely:

1. Mixing equipment.
2. Graduated delivery equipment for measurement of the medicament during filling.
3. Sealing equipment.

Area

An area of minimum twenty square meters is recommended for the basic installations.

10. Repacking of Drugs and Pharmaceutical Chemicals

The following pieces of equipment are recommended for repacking of drugs and pharmaceuticals chemicals, namely:

1. Powder disintegrator.
2. Powder sifter (electrically operated).
3. Stainless steel scoops and vessels of suitable sizes.
4. Weighing and measuring equipment.
5. Filling equipment (semi-automatic/automatic machines).
6. Electric sealing machine.

Area

An area of minimum thirty square meters is recommended for the basic installation. In case of operations involving floating particles of fine powder, a suitable exhaust system shall be provided.

11. Parenteral Preparations

The whole operation of manufacture of parenteral preparations (small volume injectables and large volume parenterals) in glass and plastic containers may be divided into the following separate areas/rooms.

11.1. ***Parenteral preparations in glass containers***

1. *Water management area*: This includes water treatment and storage.
2. *Containers and closures preparation area*: This includes washing and drying of ampoules, vials, bottles and closures.
3. *Solution preparation area*: This includes preparation and filtration of solution.
4. *Filling, capping and sealing area*: This includes filling and sealing of ampoules and/or filling, capping and sealing of vials and bottles.
5. Sterilization area.
6. Quarantine area.
7. Visual inspection area.
8. Packaging area.

The following pieces of equipment are recommended for different above mentioned areas, namely:

a. Water management area:
   1. De-ionised water treatment unit.
   2. Distillation (multi-column with heat exchangers) unit.
   3. Thermostatically controlled water storage tank.
   4. Transfer pumps.
   5. Stainless steel service lines for carrying water into user areas.

b. Containers and closures preparation area:
   1. Automatic rotary ampoule/vial/bottle washing machine having separate air, water distilled water jets.
   2. Automatic closures washing machine.
   3. Storage equipment for ampoules, vials, bottles and closures.

4. Dryer/sterilizer (double ended).
5. Dust proof storage cabinets.
6. Stainless steel benches/stools.

c. Solution preparation area:
   1. Solution preparation and mixing stainless steel tanks and other containers.
   2. Portable stirrer.
   3. Filtration equipment with cartridge and membrane filters/bacteriological filters.
   4. Transfer pumps.
   5. Stainless steel benches/stools.

d. Filling, capping and sealing area:
   1. Automatic ampoule/vial/bottle filling, sealing and capping machine under laminar airflow workstation.
   2. Gas line (nitrogen, oxygen, carbon dioxide) wherever required.
   3. Stainless steel benches/stools.

e. Sterilization area:
   1. Steam sterilizer preferably with computer control for sterilization cycle along with trolley sets for loading/unloading containers before and after sterilization).
   2. Hot air sterilizer (preferably double ended).
   3. Pressure leak test apparatus.

f. Quarantine area:
   1. Storage cabinets.
   2. Raised platforms/steel racks.

g. Visual inspection area:
   1. Visual inspection units (preferably conveyor belt type and composite white and black assembly supported with illumination).
   2. Stainless steel benches/stools.

h. Packaging area:
   1. Batch coding machine (preferably automatic).
   2. Labelling unit (preferably conveyor belt type).
   3. Benches/stools.

Area

1. A minimum area of one hundred and fifty square meters for the basic installation and an ancillary area of one hundred square meters for small volume injectables are recommended. For large volume parenterals, an area of one hundred and fifty square meters each for the basic installation and for ancillary area is recommended. These areas shall be partitioned into suitable enclosures with airlock arrangements.
2. Areas for formulations meant for external use and internal use shall be separately provided to avoid mix up.
3. Packaging materials for large volume parenteral shall have a minimum area of 100 square meters.

11.2. *Parenteral preparations in plastic containers by form-fill-seal/blow and fill-seal technology*

The whole operation of manufacture of large volume parenteral preparations in plastic containers including plastic pouches by automatic (all operations in one station) form-fill-seal machine or by semi-automatic blow moulding, filling-cum-sealing machine may be divided into following separate areas/rooms, namely:

1. Water management area.
2. Solution preparation area.
3. Containers moulding-cum-filling and sealing area.
4. Sterilization area.
5. Quarantine area.
6. Visual inspection area.
7. Packing area.

The following pieces of equipment are recommended for different above mentioned areas, namely:

a. Water management area:
   1. De-ionised water treatment unit.
   2. Distillation unit (multi-column with heat exchangers).
   3. Thermostatically controlled water storage tank.
   4. Transfer pumps.
   5. Stainless steel service lines for carrying water into user areas.

b. Solution preparation area:
    1. Solution preparation and storage tanks.
    2. Transfer pumps.
    3. Cartridge and membrane filters.
c. Container moulding-cum-filling and sealing area:
    1. Sterile form-fill-seal machine (all operations in one station with built-in laminar airflow workstation having integrated container output conveyor belt through pass box).
    2. Arrangement for feeding plastic granules through feeding-cum-filling tank into the machine.
d. *Sterilization area*: Super heated steam sterilizer (with computer control for sterilization cycle along with trolley sets for loading/unloading containers for sterilization).
e. *Quarantine area*: Adequate number of platforms/racks with storage system.
f. *Visual inspection area*: Visual inspection unit (with conveyor belt and composite
g. Packaging area:
    1. Pressure leak test apparatus (pressure belt or rotating disc type).
    2. Batch coding machine (preferably automatic).
    3. Labelling unit (preferably conveyor belt type).

Area

1. A minimum area of two hundred and fifty square meters for the basic installation of an ancillary area of one hundred and fifty square meters for large volume parenteral preparations in plastic containers by form-fill-seal technology is recommended. These areas shall be partitioned into suitable enclosures with airlock arrangements.
2. Areas for formulations meant for external use and internal use shall be separately provided to avoid mix up.
3. Packaging materials for large volume parenteral shall have a minimum area of 100 square meters.

*SCHEDUE M-I [*See* Rule 85-E (2)]

1. Requirements of Factory Premises for Manufacture of Homoeopathic Preparations

a. *Location and surroundings:* The factory shall be situated in a place which shall not be adjacent to an open sewage drain, public lavatory or any factory which produces a disagreeable or obnoxious odour or fumes or large quantities of soot, dust or smoke. The factory shall be located in a sanitary place, remove from filthy surroundings.
b. *Buildings*: The part of the building used for manufacturing shall not be used for a sleeping place and no sleeping place adjoining to it shall communicate therewith except through open air or through an intervening open space. The walls of the room in which manufacturing operations are carried out shall, up to a height of six feet from the floor, be smooth, waterproof and shall be capable of being kept clean. The flooring shall be smooth, even and washable and shall be such as not to permit retention or accumulation of dust. There shall be no chinks or crevices in the walls or floor.
c. The building used for the factory shall be constructed so as to permit production under hygienic conditions laid down in the Factories Act, 1948 (63 of 1948).
d. *Water supply:* The water used in manufacture shall be pure and drinkable quality, free from pathogenic microorganisms.
e. *Disposal of waste*: There should be adequate arrangement for disposal of wastewater and other residues from the laboratory.
f. The rooms should be airy and clean and the temperature of the room should be moderately comfortable.
g. *Health, clothing and sanitary requirements of the staff:* All workers shall be free from contagious or obnoxious disease. Their clothing shall consist of a white or coloured uniform suitable to the nature of the work and the climate, and shall be clean. Adequate facilities for personal

---

* Ins. by GOI Notification GSR No. 507(E) dt 12-06-1987 w.e.f. 12-06-1987.

cleanliness, such as clean towels, soap and hand scrubbing brushes, shall be provided separately for each sex. The workers shall be required to wash and change into clean footwear before entering the rooms where the manufacturing operations are carried on. Workers shall be required to wear either a clean cap or a suitable headgear so as to avoid any possibility of contamination by air or perspiration.

h. *Medical services:* The manufacturer shall provide adequate facilities for first aid, medical inspection of workers at the time of employment and periodically check-up thereafter at least once a year.

i. *Working benches:* Working benches shall be provided for carrying out operations such as filling, labeling, packing, etc. such benches shall be fitted with smooth, impervious tops capable of being washed.

j. *Container management*: Where operations involving use of containers such as bottles, phials and jars are conducted, there shall be adequate arrangements separated from potentisation chamber for washing, cleaning and drying such containers, with suitable equipment for the purpose. Wherever, these are attended manually adequate precaution of perfection in respect of cleanliness and avoidance of pollutants shall be taken.

2. Requirements of Plant and Equipment

a. *Mother tinctures. External tinctures and mother solution section:* The following plants and equipment shall be provided, namely:

   i. Disintegrator.
   ii. Sieved separator.
   iii. Balances and fluid measures.
   iv. Chopping boards and knives.
   v. Macerators with lids.
   vi. Percolators with lids and regulated discharge.
   vii. Moisture determination apparatus or other suitable arrangement.
   viii. Filtering arrangement.

ix. Mixing vessels and suitable non-metallic storage containers.
x. Portable stirrers.
xi. Water still.

Note

1. As for as possible metal contacts may be avoided once the drug is processed.
2. An area of 55 square meters is recommended for basic installations.
3. Adequate separate storage facility should be provided for raw material quarantine, storage and bonded room for alcohol were applicable.
4. Separate and suitable storage facility should be provided for fresh herbs and odorous raw materials.
5. Adequate laboratory facility shall be provided for testing of raw material and finished products.

b. *Potentisation section*

i. The following arrangements are recommended for container for closure preparation section, namely:
   1. Washing tanks with suitable brushing arrangement manual or mechanical.
   2. Purified water rinsing tank.
   3. Closure macerating or washing tanks.
   4. Drying chambers.
      An area of 20 square meters is recommended for basic installation.

ii. The following arrangements are recommended for potency preparation section, namely:
   1. Working tables with washable top.
   2. Facilities for separate storage of different grades of back potencies.
   3. Suitable measuring devices for discharge of drug and diluent in potentisation vial.
   4. Potentiser with counter or suitable manual arrangement.

Note

1. Different droppers shall be used for different drugs potencies.

2. All measuring devices shall be of metric system and be made of glass and shall be free from metallic contents.
3. It is desired that glass droppers, etc. intended for re-use after cleaning should be sterilized by autoclave or heating in a hot air oven.
4. Plastics, rubber tubes, bulks, etc. coming in contact with tinctures or back potencies should not be re-used for other tincture and potencies.
5. Method of potentisation will be adopted as specified in Homoeopathic Pharmacopoeia of India, Vol. I(3) Triturating, Tableting and Pill/Globules section.

3. Recommended Arrangements

i. Triturating machine for suitable device
ii. Disintegrator
iii. Mass mixer
iv. Granulator
v. Oven
vi. Tableting punches or machines
vii. Kettle (steam/gas/electrically heated) for preparation solution
viii. Dryers
ix. Sieved separator, tablet counters and balances

Note

Tablet section shall be free from dust and floating particles. An area of 55 square meters is recommended for basis installations.

4. Ointments and Lotion Section

The following arrangements are recommended, namely:

i. Mixing tank
ii. Kettle (steam, gas or electrically heated).
iii. Suitable powder mixer
iv. Ointment mill
v. Filling equipment or arrangement.

An area of 20 square meters is recommended for basic installation.

5. Syrups and Tonics

The following arrangements are recommended, namely:

i. Mixing and storage tank
ii. Potable mixer
iii. Filtering equipment
iv. Water still/deioniser
vi. Filling and sealing equipment.

An area of 20 square meters is recommended for basic installations.

6. Ophthalmic Preparations

The following pieces of equipment are recommended for manufacture under aseptic conditions of eye ointments, eye-drops, eye lotion and other preparations for external use, namely:

i. Hot air oven electrically heated with thermostatic control.
ii. Colloid mill or ointment mill.
iii. Kettle (gas or electrically heated) with suitable mixing arrangement.
iv. Tube filling equipment.
v. Mixing and storage tanks of stainless steel or of other suitable material.
vi. Sintered glass funnel, Seitz filter or filter candle.
vii. Liquid filling equipment
viii. Autoclaves

Adequate precaution should be taken to ensure that the finished product is sterile. An area of 20 square meters is recommended for basic installations.

7. Adequate Arrangements for Space and Equipment should Made for Labeling and Packing

** SCHEDULE M-II [*See* Rule 139]

I. Requirement of Factory Premises for Manufacture of Cosmetics

1. General Requirements

a. *Location and surroundings:* The factory shall be located in a sanitary place and hygienic conditions shall be maintained in the premises. Premises shall not be used for residence or be interconnected with residential area. It shall be well ventilated and clean.

b. *Buildings:* The buildings used for the factory shall be constructed so as to permit production under hygienic conditions and not to permit entry of insects, rodents, files, etc. The walls of the room in which manufacturing operations are carried out, shall up to a height of six feet from the floor, be smooth, waterproof and capable of being kept clean. The flooring shall be smooth, even and washable and shall be such as not to permit retention or accumulation of dust.

c. *Water supply*: The water used in manufacture shall be of potable quality.

d. *Disposal of water:* Suitable arrangements shall be made for disposal of wastewater.

e. *Health, clothing and sanitary requirements of the staff:* All workers shall be free from contagious or infectious diseases. They shall be provided with clean uniforms, masks, headgears, and gloves wherever required. Washing facilities shall also be provided.

f. *Medical services:* Adequate facilities for first aid shall be provided.

g. Working benches shall be provided for carrying out operations such as filling, labeling, packing, etc. such benches shall be fitted with smooth, impervious tops capable of being washed.

h. Adequate facilities shall be provided for washing and drying of glass containers if the same are to be used for packing the product.

** Ins. by GOI Notification No. GSR 723(E) dt 11-8-1992.

II. Requirements of Plant and Equipment

The following equipment, area and other requirements are recommended for the manufacture of following products:

A. Powders

Face powder, cake make-up, compacts, face packs, masks, rouges, etc.

Equipment

a. Powder mixer of suitable type provided with a dust collector.
b. Perfume and colour blender.
c. Sifter with sieves of suitable mesh size.
d. Ball mill or suitable grinder.
e. Trays and scoops (stainless steel).
f. Filling and sealing equipment provided with dust extractor.
g. For compacts:
   i. A separate mixer.
   ii. Compact pressing machine.
h. Weighing and measuring devices.
i. Storage tanks.

An area of 15 square meters is recommended. The section is to be provided with adequate exhaust fans.

B. Creams, Lotions, Emulsions, Pastes, Cleansing Milks, Shampoos, Pomade, Brilliantine, Shaving Creams and Hair-oils

a. Mixing and storage tanks of suitable materials.
b. Heating kettle steam, gas or electrically heated.
c. Suitable agitator.
d. Colloidal mill or homogeniser (wherever necessary).
e. Triple roller mill (wherever necessary).
f. Filling and sealing equipment.
g. Weighing and measuring devices.

An area of 25 square meters is recommended.

C. Nail Polishes and Nail Lacquers

1. *Equipment*
   a. A suitable mixer.
   b. Storage tanks.
   c. Filling machine—hand operated or power driven.
   d. Weighing and measuring devices.

   An area of 15 square meters is recommended. The section shall be provided with flameproof exhaust system.
2. *Premises:* The following are the special requirements related to nail polishes and nail lacquers:
   a. It shall be suited in an industrial area.
   b. It shall be separate from other cosmetic-manufacturing areas by metal/brick partition up to ceiling.
   c. Floors, walls, ceiling and doors shall be fireproof.
   d. Smoking, cooking and dwelling shall not be permitted and no naked flame shall be brought in the premises.
   e. All electrical writing and connections shall be concealed and main electric switch shall be outside the manufacturing area.
   f. All equipment, furniture and light fittings in the section shall be flameproof.
   g. Fire extinguisher like foam and dry powder and sufficient number of buckets containing and shall be provided.
   h. All doors of the section shall open outwards.
3. *Storage:* All explosive solvents and ingredients shall be stored in metal cupboards or in a separate enclosed area.
4. *Manufacture*
   a. Manufacture of lacquers shall not be undertaken unless the above conditions are complied with.
   b. Workers shall be asked to wear shoes with rubber soles in the section.
5. *Other requirements:* No objection certificate from the local Fire Brigade Authorities shall be furnished.

D. Lipsticks and Lip-gloss

Equipment

a. Vertical mixer.
b. Jacketted kettle, steam, gas or electrically heated.
c. Mixing vessel (stainless steel).
d. Triple roller mill/ball mill.
e. Moulds with refrigeration facility.
f. Weighing and measuring devices.

An area of 15 square meters is recommended.

E. Depilatories

Equipment

a. Mixing tanks.
b. Mixer.
c. Triple roller mill or homogeniser (wherever necessary).
d. Filling and sealing equipment.
e. Weighing and measuring devices.
f. Moulds (wherever necessary).

An area of 10 square meters is recommended.

F. Preparations used for Eyes

Such preparations shall be manufactured under strict hygienic conditions to ensure that these are safe for use.

1. *Eyebrows, Eyelashes, and Eyeliners*

Equipment

a. Mixing tanks.
b. A suitable mixer.
c. Homogeniser (wherever necessary)
d. Filling and sealing equipment.
e. Weighing and measuring devices.

An area of 10 square meters is recommended.

2. *Kajal and Surma*

Equipment

a. Base sterilizer
b. Powder sterilizer (dry heat oven).

c. Stainless steel tanks.
d. A suitable mixer.
e. Stainless steel sieves.
f. Filling and sealing arrangements.
g. Weighing and measuring devices.
h. Homogeniser (wherever necessary).
i. Pestle and Mortar (for Surma).

An area of 10 square meters with a separate area of 5 square meters for base sterilization is recommended. Other requirements for 1 and 2

a. False ceiling shall be provided wherever required.
b. Manufacturing area shall be made fly proof. An airlock or an air curtain shall be provided.
c. Base used for Kajal shall be sterilized by heating the base at 150°C for required time in a separate enclosed area.
d. The vegetable carbon black powder shall be sterilized in a drying oven at 120 °C for required time.
e. All utensils used for manufacture shall be of stainless steel and shall be washed with detergent water, antiseptic liquid and again with distilled water.
f. Containers employed for Kajal shall be cleaned properly with bactericidal solution and dried.
g. Workers shall put on clean overalls and use hand gloves wherever necessary.

G. Aerosol

Equipment

a. Air compressor (wherever necessary).
b. Mixing tanks.
c. Suitable propellant filling and crimping equipments.
d. Liquid filling unit.
e. Leak testing equipment.
f. Fire extinguisher (wherever necessary)
g. Suitable filtration equipment.
h. Weighing and measuring devices.

An area of 15 square meters is recommended.

Other requirements: No objection certificate from the Local Fire Brigade Authorities shall be furnished.

H. Alcoholic Fragrance Solutions

Equipment

a. Mixing tanks with stirrer.
b. Filtering equipment.
c. Filling and sealing equipment.
d. Weighing and measuring devices.

An area of 15 square meters is recommended.

I. Hair Dyes

Equipment

a. Stainless steel tanks.
b. Mixer.
c. Filling unit.
d. Weighing and measuring devices.
e. Masks, gloves and goggles.

An area of 15 square meters with proper exhaust is recommended.

J. Toothpowders and Toothpastes

1. *Toothpowder in general*

Equipment

a. Weighing and measuring devices.
b. Dry mixer (powder blender).
c. Stainless steel sieves.
d. Powder filling and sealing equipment.

An area of 15 square meters with proper exhaust is recommended.

2. *Toothpastes*

Equipment

a. Weighing and measuring devices.
b. Kettle steam, gas or electrically heated (where necessary)
c. Planetory mixer with de-aerator system.
d. Stainless steel tanks.

e. Tube filling equipment.
f. Crimping machine.

An additional area of 15 square meters with proper exhaust is recommended.

3. *Toothpowder (black)*

Equipment

a. Weighing and measuring devices.
b. Dry mixer powder blender.
c. Stainless steel sieves.
d. Powder filling arrangements.

An area of 15 square meters with proper exhaust is recommended. Areas for manufacturing black and white toothpowders should be separate.

K. Toilet Soaps

Equipment

a. Kettles/pans for saponification.
b. Boiler or any other suitable heating arrangement.
c. Suitable stirring arrangement.
d. Storage tanks or trays.
e. Driers.
f. Amalgamator/chipping machine.
g. Mixer.
h. Triple roller mill.
i. Granulator.
j. Plodder.
k. Cutter.
l. Pressing, stamping and embossing machine.
m. Weighing and measuring devices.

A minimum area of 100 square meters is recommended for the small-scale manufacture of toilet soaps. The areas recommended above are for basic manufacturing of different categories of cosmetics. In addition to that separate adequate space for storage of raw materials, finished products, packing materials shall be provided in factory premises.

Note No. I. The above requirements of the schedule are made subject to modification at the direction of the licensing authority, if he is of the opinion that having regard to the nature and extent of the manufacturing operations, it is necessary to relax or alter them in the circumstances of a particular case.

Note No. II. The above requirements do not include requirements of machinery, equipment and premises required for preparation of containers and closers of different categories of cosmetics. The licensing authority shall have the discretion to examine the suitability and adequacy of the machinery, equipment and premises for the purpose of taking into consideration of the requirements of the licence.

Note No. III. Schedule M-II specifies equipment and space required for certain categories of cosmetics only. There are other cosmetics items, viz. attars, perfumes, etc., which are not covered in the above categories. The licensing authority shall, in respect of such items or the words. A testing laboratory shall also be provided, were omitted by GOI Notification No. GSR 285 (E), dt 16.07.1996. Categories of cosmetics have the discretion to examine the adequacy of factory premises, space, plant and machinery and other requisites having regard to the nature and extent of the manufacturing operations involved and direct the licensee to carry on necessary modification in them.

Note No. IV. Areas for formulations meant for external use and areas for formulations meant for internal use shall be separately provided to avoid mix-up even though they are from the same category of formulations.

***SCHEDULE M-III [*See Rule 76*]

Requirements of Factory Premises for Manufacture of Medical Devices

1. General Requirements

1.1. *Location and surroundings:* The factory building(s) shall be located in a sanitary place and hygienic conditions shall be

*** Ins. by GOI Notification No. GSR 109(E), w.e.f. 22-2-1994.

maintained in the premises. Premises shall be not used for residence or be interconnected with residence. It shall be well ventilated and clean.

1.2. ***Buildings:*** The buildings used for the factory shall be constructed so as to permit production under hygienic conditions and not to permit entry of insets, rodents, flies, etc. The walls of the rooms in which manufacturing operations are carried out, shall be up to a height of six feet from the floor, be smooth, waterproof and capable of being kept clean. The floor shall be smooth, even and washable and shall be such as not to permit retention or accumulation of dust.

1.3. ***Water supply:*** The water used in manufacture shall be of potable quality.

1.4. ***Disposal of waste:*** Suitable arrangements shall be made for disposal of wastewater.

1.5. ***Health, clothing and sanitation of workers:*** All workers shall be free from contagious or infectious diseases. They shall be provided with clean uniforms, masks, headgears and gloves wherever required. Washing facilities shall also be provided.

1.6. ***Medical services:*** Adequate facilities for first aid shall be provided.

1.7. Workbenches shall be provided for carrying out operations such as moulding, assembling, labeling, packing, etc., such benches shall be fitted with smooth impervious tops capable of being washed.

1.8. Adequate facilities shall be provided wherever required for cleaning, washing, drying of different containers of devices.

1.9. The premises shall be kept under controlled conditions of temperature and humidity so as to prevent any deterioration in the properties of materials and products due to storage and process conditions.

2. Requirements for Manufacture of Medical Devices

The process of manufacture of medical devices shall be conducted at the licensed premises, wherever required, and shall be divided into the following separate operations/sections:

1. Moulding (wherever manufacture of medical devices is to start from granules).

2. Assembling (include cutting, washing and drying, sealing, packing, labeling, etc.).
3. Raw materials.
4. Storage area.
5. Washing, drying and sealing area (wherever required).
6. Sterilization.
7. Testing facilities.

The following equipment and space are recommended for the basic manufacture of different categories of medical devices.

A. Sterile Disposable Perfusion and Blood Collection Sets

Moulding

a. Injection moulding machine.
b. Extruder machine.
c. PVC resin compounding machine.

Assembling

a. Hand pressing machine for filter fixing a drip chamber.
b. Bag sealing machine.
c. Compressor machine.
d. Leak testing bench.
e. PVC tube cutting machine.
f. Tube winding machine (wherever necessary).
g. Welding machine (wherever necessary).

An area of 30 square meters for moulding and 15 square meters for assembling is recommended for basic installation. The assembling area shall be air-conditioned provided with HEPA filters. The moulding section shall, if necessary, have proper exhaust system.

Note: *An additional area of 20 square meters is recommended for any extra category.*

B. Sterile Disposable Hypodermic Syringes

Moulding

a. Granulator
b. Injection moulding machine
c. Weighing devices

Assembling

a. Blister pack machine.
b. Vacuum dust cleaner.
c. Rubber-tip washing machine.
d. Foil stamping or screen printing equipment.

An area of 30 square meters for moulding and 15 square metres for assembling are recommended for basic installation. The assembling area shall be air-conditioned provided with HEPA filters. The moulding section, shall, if necessary, have proper exhaust system.

Note: *An additional area of 20 square meters is recommended for any extra category.*

C. Sterile Disposable Hypodermic Needles

Moulding

a. Needle grinding and leveling machine.
b. Electro-polishing machine.
c. Cutting machine.
d. Injection moulding machine.
e. Needle pointing deburrine machine.
f. Air compressor.

Assembling

a. Needle cleaning machine with magnetic separator.
b. Blister packing machine.
c. Needle inspection unit.

An area of 30 square meters for moulding and 15 square meters for assembling are recommended for basic installation. The assembling area shall be air-conditioned provided with HEPA filters. The moulding section shall, if necessary, have proper exhaust system.

Note: *An additional area of 20 square meters is recommended for any extra category.*

3. Raw Materials

The licensee shall keep an inventory of all raw materials to be used at any stage of manufacture of devices and shall maintain records as per Schedule U. All such raw materials shall be identified and assigned control reference number. They shall be conspicuously labeled indicating the name of the material, control reference number, name of the manufacturer and be specially labeled under test or approved or rejected. The under test, approved or rejected materials shall appropriately be segregated. These shall be tested for compliance with required standards of quality. A minimum area of 10 square meters shall be provided for storage of raw materials.

4. Storage Area

The licensee shall provide separate storage facilities for quarantine and sterilized products. An area not less than 10 square metres shall be provided for each of them.

5. Washing, Drying and Sealing Area

The licensee shall provide wherever required adequate equipment like water distillation still, deionizer, washing machine. Drying oven with trays for washing, drying and sealing of medical device. An area not less than 10 square metres shall be provided.

6. Sterilization

The licensee shall provide requisite equipment with required controls and recording device for sterilization of medical devices by ethylene oxide gas in his own premises or may make arrangements with some institution approved by the Licensing Authority for sterilization. The products sterilized in this manner shall be monitored to assure acceptable levels of residual gas and its degradation products. An area of 10 square meters is recommended for basic installation of such facility. Provided that the above equipment may not be required in case the licensee opts for sterilization of medical devices by ionising radiation.

7. Testing Facilities

The licensee shall provide testing laboratory for carrying out chemical and physiochemical testing of medical devices and of raw materials used in its own premises. Provided that the Licensing Authority shall permit the licensee in the initial stage to carry out testing of sterility, pyrogens, toxicity on their products from the approved testing institutions but after one renewal period of licensee shall provide testing facilities of all such tests in their own premises.

8. Records

The licensee shall maintain records of different manufacturing activities with regard to each stage of manufacture in-process control, assembling, packing, batch records for the quantity of devices manufactured from each lot of blended granules, duration of work, hourly quantum of production in respect of each item as well as record of each sterilizing cycle of the gaseous method employed.

> ***Note:*** *The above requirements of machinery, equipment, space, qualifications are made subject to the modification at the discretion of the Licensing Authority, if he is of the opinion that having regard to the nature and extent of the manufacturing operations it is necessary to relax or alter them in the circumstances of a particular case.*

9

Economic Capacity, Project Cost & Profitability Projection of Acts

Economic capacity	240 tonnes per annum
Project cost	Rs. 215 lakhs

Assessment of project cost

S. No.	*Description*	*Cost (Rs. in lakhs)*
1.	**Land**	
	1.1 Cost of land of one acre at Rs. 5.5 lakh per acre	5.50
	1.2 Cost of levelling, laying internal roads/fencing and compound wall	0.55
	Subtotal	6.05
2.	**Building**	
	2.1 Factory building of area 620 sqm at Rs. 3200/sqm	19.84
	2.2 Non-factory building of area 60 sqm at Rs. 4500/sqm	2.70
	Subtotal	22.54
3.	**Cost of plant and machinery**	
	3.1 Cost of basic plant and machinery	75 .00
	3.2 Instrumentation and control	5.63
	3.3 Pipelines and valves	7.50
	3.4 Structurals for erection	3.75
	Subtotal	91.88
	3.5 Octroi, excise duty, sales tax, etc. at 12%	11.03
	3.6 Packaging and insurance charges (2%)	1.84
	3.7 Transportation charges (2%)	1.84
	3.8 Machinery stores and spares (2%)	1.84
	3.9 Foundation charges (2%)	1.84
	3.10 Installation charges (2%)	1.84
	Total cost of plant and machinery	112.11

(Contd.)

S. No.	Description	Cost (Rs. in lakhs)
4.	**Technical know-how fees** Rs. 2.5 lakhs	20.00
5.	**Miscellaneous fixed assets**	
	5.1 Electrification	4.00
	5.2 Steam boiler and auxillaries	4.00
	5.3 Water storage tank, borewell, etc.	1.00
	5.4 Fuel storage tank	2.00
	5.5 Laboratory equipment	0.80
	5.6 Office machinery and equipment	1.60
	5.7 Material handling equipment, packaging machinery, weigh balance, etc.	1.50
	5.8 Diesel generator	4.50
	5.9 Effluent treatment	1.40
	Total	20.80
6.	**Preliminary and preoperative expenses**	
	6.1 Preliminary expenses	0.80
	6.2 Preoperative expenses:	
	6.2.1 Establishment	0.80
	6.2.2 Rent rates and taxes	0.80
	6.2.3 Travelling expenses	1.20
	6.2.4 Interest and commitment charges on borrowings	7.20
	6.2.5 Insurance during construction period	3.50
	6.2.6 Other preoperative expenses and deposits	–
	6.2.7 Interest on deferred payment	–
	Total	14.3
7.	**Provision for contingency**	11.17
8.	**Working capital margin**	26.25
9.	**Total project cost**	215.00
10.	**Means of finance**	
	• Promoter's contribution	86.00
	• Term loan from financing institutions	129.00
	• Total project cost	215.00
11.	**Financial statements**	
	Cost of production	
	A. *Variable cost*	
	• Raw material and utilities	194.32
	• Spares and maintenance	6.73
	• Selling expenses	17.76
	Total variable cost (A)	218.81

(Contd.)

S. No.	Description	Cost (Rs. in lakhs)
	B. *Fixed cost*	
	• Salaries and wages	18.00
	• Interest on term loan and working capital loan	37.38
	• Depreciation	14.46
	Administrative expenses	10.66
	Total fixed cost (B)	80.50
	C. *Total cost of production* (A + B)	299.11
	D. *Selling price* (in Rupees)—148.00/kg	
	E. *Annual sales turnover*	355.20
	F. *Net profit before tax* (E – C)	55.89
	G. *Break-even point*—59%	

10

Financial Outlay of Act

A. Plant and Machinery

S. No.	Description of plant and machinery	Qty.	Value (Rs.)
1.	Pulveriser with 7.5 HP and 2.5 HP motor	1	60000.00
2.	Disintegrator with 7.5 HP size with sieve of different mesh size	1	56000.00
3.	Wooden vessel for fermentation with lid, cap. 50 L	25	70000.00
4.	MS Vat cap 750 kg	1	50000.00
5.	Earthen pots with lid for *Bhasma* production cap. 2 kg	12	40000.00
6.	Tableting machine	1	80000.00
7.	Bottle filling machine	1	15000.00
8.	Bottle sealing machine	1	10000.00
9.	SS mixing vessel with stirrer cap. 200 L	1	70000.00
10.	MS pastle and motor	1	45000.00
11.	Water treatment/distillation plant	1	10000.00
12.	Earthen vatti	5	4000.00
13.	Weighing scale 100 kg cap.	1	10000.00
14.	Weighing scale 5 kg cap.	1	5000.00
15.	Filtering unit fitted with paper and cloth	1	40000.00
16.	Cane, bamboo baskets, flass jar big and small with stopper	25 each	45000.00
17.	SS vessel with stopper 5 L cap.	1	5000.00
	10 L cap.	1	10000.00
	100 L cap.	1	20000.00
18.	Hot air oven with 24 trays 0.5 HP motor	1	60000.00
19.	Bottle washing and drying machine	1 each	20000.00
20.	Aluminum containers for storage of powders/raw materials	50	20000.00
21.	Firefighting and pollution control equipment	1	80000.00
22.	Testing equipment		30000.00
23.	Erection and electrification at 10% pa		85000.00
24.	Total		9,40,000.00

B. Furniture, Fixture, Almirah, Computer, etc. = Rs. 60,000

Staff and Labour (pm)

S. No.	*Designation*	*No.*	*Salary (Rs.)*
1.	Manager-cum-manufacturing chemist	1	10000
2.	Analytical chemist	1	7000
3.	Clerk-cum-accountant	1	5000
4.	Skilled worker	2	8000
5.	Unskilled worker	3	9000
6.	Peon-cum-chowkidar	1	4000
7.	Sales representative	1	8000
	Total:		51000
	Perquisite at 15% pa		7650
	Total		58650

Raw Materials (pm)

Raw materials are different type of herbal plants, mineral, sugar, honey, *bhasma* etc. are available indigenously and consumables including packaging materials like glass bottles, paper containers, etc. are available in the Haryana and nearest states and it will be of estimated value of Rs. 2.5 lacs.

Other Expenses (pm)

	Value (in Rs.)
Utilities	
Power	4000
Wood/Coal	2000
Water	500
Rent	5000
Postage and stationery	500
Traveling and transport charge	2000
Advt. and publicity	500
Repair and maintenance	500
Insurance	500
Consumables store	500
Micellaneous	500
Total	17000

Total Recurring Expenses (pm)

	In Rupees
Raw material	2,50000
Staff and labour	58650
Other expenses	17000
Total	3,25,650

Fixed capital	= Rs. 9,40,000 + Rs. 60000 = Rs.10,00000
Working capital for three months	= Rs. 3,25,650 × 3 = Rs. 9,76,950
Total capital investment	= Rs. 9,76,950 + Rs.10,00000 = Rs. 19,76,950

Cost of Production (pa)

	In Rupees
Recurring exp.	39,07,800
Depreciation on plant and Mc at 10% pa	94000
Depreciation on furniture at 25% pa	15000
Interest on TCI at 18% pa	3,55,851
Total	43,72,651

Turn-over by Sale

S. No.	*Item*	*Qty.*	*Packing/ bottle*	*Rate (in Rupees per piece)*	*Value (in Rupees)*
1.	Ashokaristha	30000	750 ml bottle	50	15,00000
2.	Lakhibilas ras	20000	10 gm bottle	50	10,00000
3.	Lavanbhaskar churna	60000	100 gm pkt	20	12,00000
4.	Chayanpras	3000	1 kg box	170	5,10,000
5.	Mritsanjivni	10000	300 ml bottle	50	5,00000
6.	Gandhkadi mahlam	18000	10 gm box	50	9,00000
7.	Sitapaladi churna	3000	100 gm box	50	1,50,000
	Total				57,60,000

Profit per year	= Rs. 57,60,000 – Rs. 43,72,651 = Rs.13,87,349
Less 10% discount to stockiest, dealers, etc.	= Rs. 13,87,349 – Rs.1,38,734 = Rs. 12,48,615
Net profit/year	= Rs. 12,48,615
Percentage profit on sale	= Rs. 12,48,615 × 100 = 21.67% = Rs. 57,60,000
Percentage profit on total capital investment	= Rs. 12,48,615 × 100 = 63.15% = Rs. 19,76,950/-

Break-even Point

Fixed cost (in Rupees):	
40% of salary and wages	2,81,520
40% of other expenses	81,600
Total depreciation on plant and Mc, furniture, etc.	1,09,000
Interest on total capital investment at 18% pa	3,55,851
Total:	8,27,971

BEP = FC × 100 = Rs. 8,27,971 × 100
FC + profit Rs. 8,27,971 + Rs. 12,48,615 = 39.87%

Addresses of Raw Material Suppliers

1. M/s Bridhishand Keshab Deo
   Gancy Bazar
   Guwahati-1.
2. M/s Debendra Nath Dutt & Sons
   Debendra Bhavan, 13 Cotton Street
   Calcutta-1.
3. Co-operative Drug Factory of Ranikhet
   Ranikhet (UP)
4. Local dealers in herbs, medicinal plants, etc.

Addresses of Machinery and Equipment Suppliers

1. M/s Techno Fill Pvt. Ltd.
   BP 49, Neelam Bata Road
   Faribadbad-121001

2. M/s Strip India
   16 Mandal Temple Road, P-Block
   New Alipore, Calcutta-53
3. M/s Cadmach Machinery Co. Pvt. Ltd.
   P.O. Box No. 9007
   Naningar
   Ahmedabad-380008
4. M/s Modern Mechanical Works
   1501, Qsim Jon Street
   Delhi-6
5. M/s Associated Instrument Manufacturing Pvt. Ltd.
   26, Asaf Ali Road
   New Delhi-6
6. M/s Pharmaceutical Machinery Manufacturing Works
   Laxmi Nagar, Indl. Estate
   Indore-4
7. M/s Emkay (India) Trading Co.
   286, Garhiaya, Jama Masjid
   New Delhi-6

Bibliography

1. Drugs and Cosmetics Formulations, CBS Publishers and Distributors, New Delhi, Ranjan Magazine.
2. Drugs and Cosmetics Act 1940 and Rules 1945, CBS Publishers and Distributors, New Delhi, Ranjan Magazine.
3. www.google.com

Index